CASTLES&
CATHEDRALS

getmapping® + HarperCollins*Publishers*

CASTLES&
CATHEDRALS

100 AMAZING VIEWS FROM
www.getmapping.com

Contents

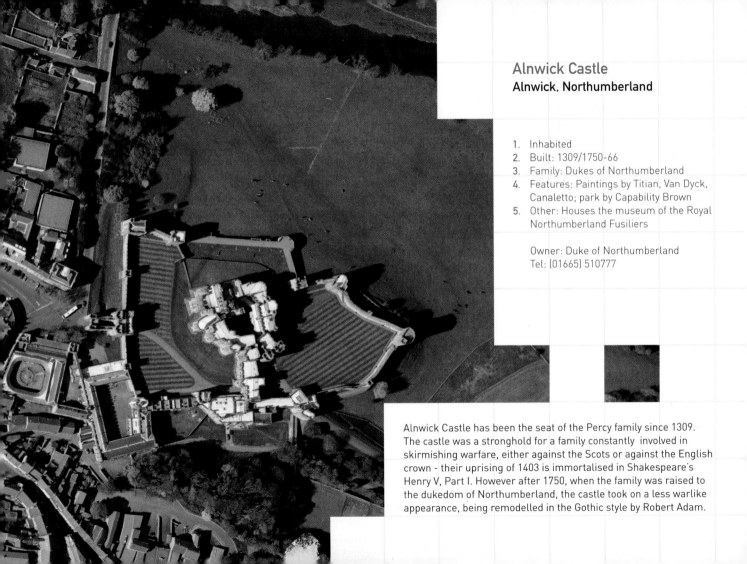

Alnwick Castle
Alnwick, Northumberland

1. Inhabited
2. Built: 1309/1750-66
3. Family: Dukes of Northumberland
4. Features: Paintings by Titian, Van Dyck, Canaletto; park by Capability Brown
5. Other: Houses the museum of the Royal Northumberland Fusiliers

Owner: Duke of Northumberland
Tel: (01665) 510777

Alnwick Castle has been the seat of the Percy family since 1309. The castle was a stronghold for a family constantly involved in skirmishing warfare, either against the Scots or against the English crown - their uprising of 1403 is immortalised in Shakespeare's Henry V, Part I. However after 1750, when the family was raised to the dukedom of Northumberland, the castle took on a less warlike appearance, being remodelled in the Gothic style by Robert Adam.

Arundel Castle
Arundel, West Sussex

1. Inhabited
2. Built: Norman/19th century
3. Built for: Montgomery, Earl of Shrewsbury
4. Features: Paintings by Gainsborough, Holbein, Van Dyck; Fitzalan Chapel (1380), Baron's Hall
5. Other: Taken by Henry I in 1102, and by Parliamentarian Sir William Waller, Civil War 1643; two of the 3rd Duke's nieces, Anne Boleyn and Catherine Howard, married Henry VIII; Hiorn's Tower, built in 1790, stands in the 1100-acre grounds like a medieval hunting-tower

Owner: Duke of Norfolk
Tel: (01903) 883136

In 1749 Horace Walpole described Arundel Castle as "now only a heap of ruins, with a new indifferent apartment clapt up for the Norfolks when they reside there for a week or a fortnight", but the castle was restored in the 1780s and rebuilt again at the end of the 19th century by the 15th Duke.

Bamburgh Castle
Bamburgh, Northumberland

1. Restored
2. Built: 1207-72/1903
3. Family: Crown/Lord Armstrong
4. Features: Collection of armour; Fabergé carvings; double-towered east gate
5. Other: Taken during the Wars of the Roses, by the Earl of Warwick for Edward IV; haunted by a knight in full armour; already a ruin by Tudor times but restored by Lord Armstrong, 1894-1903

Owner: Francis Armstrong
Tel: (01668) 214515

During the Wars of the Roses Bamburgh became the first castle in England to be breached by gunfire - the two cannon responsible were called Newcastle and Dyson. Surrender came after a hole was blown in the castle walls, although capitulation cannot have been far off even without the cannon fire because the garrison had already eaten all of its horses.

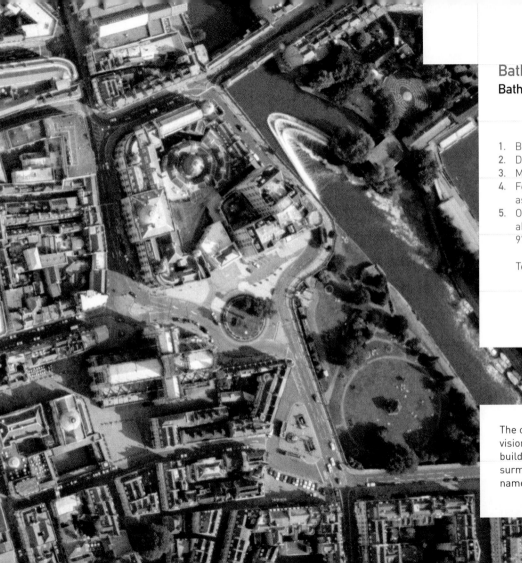

Bath Abbey
Bath, Somerset

1. Built: 1499/17th century
2. Dedicated to: St Peter and St Paul
3. Monastic order: Benedictine
4. Features: West Front carvings of angels ascending and descending from heaven
5. Other: Built on the site of the Saxon abbey where King Edgar was crowned in 973

Tel: (01225) 422462

The carvings on the West Front recall the vision that inspired Bishop Oliver King to build the abbey, and carvings of olive trees surmounted by crowns are a play on his name

Battle Abbey
Battle, East Sussex

1. Built: 1070/1338
2. Dedicated to: St Martin
3. Monastic order: Benedictine
4. Features: Huge gatehouse, added in 1338
5. Other: Dissolved by Henry VIII; the gatehouse contains an audio-visual exhibition on the Battle of Hastings

Owner: English Heritage
Tel: (01424) 773792

The town of Battle, not Hastings itself, was the site of the Battle of Hastings in 1066, and before the battle William vowed that should he win he would build a religious foundation on the spot where Harold fell. True to his word he built Battle Abbey which became home to a fraternity of Benedictine monks.

Beaumaris Castle
Beaumaris, Anglesey

1. Ruin
2. Built: 1295-1312
3. Built for: Edward I
4. Features: 16ft thick walls in concentric rings
5. Other: Never saw action; surrendered without a fight to Major-General Mytton, Civil War 1646; the name derives from beau marais, meaning beautiful marsh, supposedly so named to attract English settlers

Owner: Cadw, Welsh Historic Monuments
Tel: (01248) 810361

The main entrance to the outer ward of the castle is called the "Gate next the Sea", and beside it, on the south side of the castle, is a dock which ships could use at high tide – a useful way of replenishing supplies during a seige.

Belvoir Castle
Belvoir, Leicestershire

1. Inhabited
2. Built: 1816
3. Built by: James Wyatt
4. Features: Paintings by Van Dyck, Murillo, Holbein
5. Other: Contains the museum of the Queen's Royal Lancers; the Belvoir foxhound is named after the castle

Owner: Duke of Rutland
Tel: (01476) 870262

Belvoir Castle has been described as "an incoherent castellated pile" having been rebuilt several times, most recently in the early 19th century as a sham medieval castle. The castle contains Hans Holbein's famous portrait of Henry VIII – Holbein managed to please the vain king by treading a delicate line between honesty and flattery in his portraiture.

Bodiam Castle
2 miles E of Bodiam, East Sussex

1. Ruin
2. Built: 1386
3. Built for: Sir Edward Dalyngrigge
4. Features: Guards the River Rother
5. Other: Attacked during the Wars of the Roses 1484 and surrendered without siege in the Civil War, 1643; restored in the 20th century by Lord Curzon, who found 28 lavatories built into the walls with drainage into the moat

Owner: National Trust
Tel: (01580) 830436

The defences at Bodiam were particularly ingenious, including the approach across the octagonal island in the lake. Originally this small island was fortified, and approach to it was by a wooden bridge at right-angles to the castle, forcing any attacking forces to expose their right flank to the defending garrison.

Bolsover Castle
Castle St, Bolsover, Derbyshire

1. Ruin
2. Built: c1612
3. Built for: Sir Charles Cavendish
4. Features: Keep by Robert Smythson
5. Other: Indoor Riding School dating from
   the 17th century

   Owner: English Heritage
   Tel: (01246) 823349

Bolsover Castle is built on land given by William the
Conqueror to William Peveril, the builder of Peveril
Castle in Derbyshire. The original castle no longer
exists, though – what stands in its place is an early
example of a fashion for sham medieval castles, and
was built in the 17th century.

Bradford Cathedral
Bradford, West Yorkshire

1. Built: 15th/20th century
2. Dedicated to: St Peter
3. Architect: 20th century additions by Sir Edward Maufe
4. Height of tower: 100ft
5. Features: William Morris glass, sculpture by Flaxman and Shaw; foursquare Tudor tower; freestanding organ
6. Other: Became a cathedral in 1919; restored 1951

Tel: (01274) 777720

The bells of Bradford Cathedral were recast in 1921 as a memorial to the fallen of the First World War.

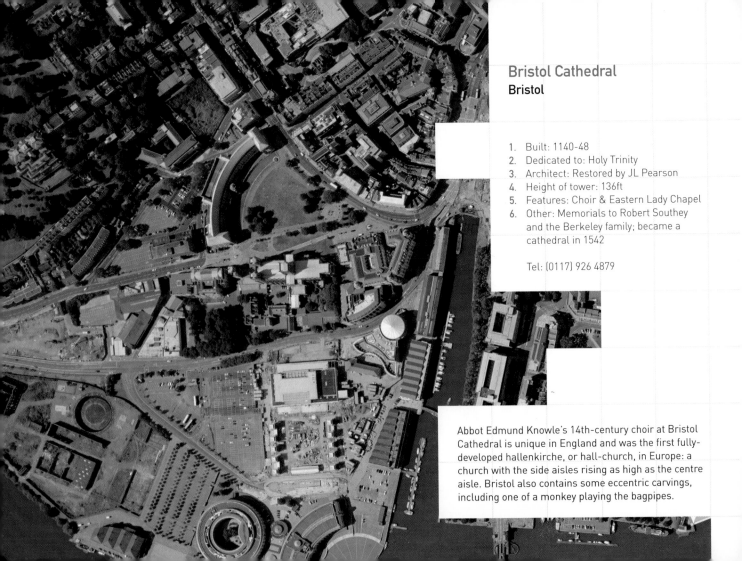

Bristol Cathedral
Bristol

1. Built: 1140-48
2. Dedicated to: Holy Trinity
3. Architect: Restored by JL Pearson
4. Height of tower: 136ft
5. Features: Choir & Eastern Lady Chapel
6. Other: Memorials to Robert Southey and the Berkeley family; became a cathedral in 1542

Tel: (0117) 926 4879

Abbot Edmund Knowle's 14th-century choir at Bristol Cathedral is unique in England and was the first fully-developed hallenkirche, or hall-church, in Europe: a church with the side aisles rising as high as the centre aisle. Bristol also contains some eccentric carvings, including one of a monkey playing the bagpipes.

Broughty Castle
4 miles E of Dundee, Angus

1. Restored
2. Built: 1490s/1861
3. Built for: Andrew, 3rd Lord Gray
4. Features: Local history exhibits; built to protect the estuary.
5. Other: Treacherously delivered to the English, 1547; regained by Scots and French 1550; taken by General Monck for Cromwell, 1651; Alexander Leslie was imprisoned here

Owner: Historic Scotland/run by Dundee City Council
Tel: (01382) 436916

Although Broughty Castle was in ruins by 1820, it was bought by the government in 1851 and restored ten years later by architect Sir Robert Rowand Anderson. The castle was equipped with new gun emplacements and was used until after the Second World War – it now houses a museum of local history, whaling, fishery and arms and armour.

Buckfast Abbey
1 mile N of Buckfastleigh, Devon

1. Built: 1907-32
2. Dedicated to: St Mary
3. Monastic order: Benedictine
4. Features: Stained glass designed and made by the monks who restored the abbey; 14th century guest hall
5. Other: The guest hall contains an exhibition on the history of the abbey

Tel: (01364) 645500

Buckfast Abbey was reconsecrated in 1932, having been rebuilt by four exiled French Benedictine monks on the foundations of a Cistercian abbey that was razed by Henry VIII in 1535. The original abbey was founded in 1018 by King Canute.

Caernarfon Castle
Caernarfon, Gwynedd

1. Ruin
2. Built: 1283-1328
3. Built for: Edward I
4. Features: Museum of Royal Welch Fusiliers; polygonal towers, including the 124ft 10-sided Eagle Tower
5. Other: Withstood two sieges by Owain Glyndwr; fell to Parliamentarian Major-General Mytton, Civil War 1646; Edward I's son and heir born here 1284; investiture of Prince Charles as Prince of Wales, 1969; said to be copied from the Theodosian walls of Constantinople, reflecting a tradition that Constantine was born nearby

Owner: Cadw, Welsh Historic Monuments
Tel: (01286) 677617

When a son was born to Edward I at Caernarfon in 1284, the king is said to have presented the new-born to the Welsh people as their prince and future king, saying that he was blameless – born on Welsh soil and speaking not a word of English. The story is probably not true but the prince was invested as Prince of Wales in 1301, a title that has since been traditionally conferred on the monarch's eldest son.

Caerphilly Castle
Caerphilly, Mid-Glamorgan

1. Partially restored
2. Built: 1268-1326
3. Built for: Gilbert de Clare
4. Features: The south-east tower leans at a steeper angle than the tower at Pisa
5. Other: Besieged by Queen Isabella while she was pursuing Edward II; captured by Owain Glyndwr, 15th century; the largest castle in Wales; built as a defence against Llywelyn the Last

Owner: Cadw, Welsh Historic Monuments
Tel: (029) 2088 3143

There are several theories as to the origin of the Leaning Tower of Caerphilly, ranging from subsidence or Civil War damage to the machinations of the evil Queen Isabella. The tower contained a furnace used for producing molten lead to pour on the enemy during sieges, and it is said that, while pursuing her husband Edward II, Queen Isabella's soldiers captured the tower and attempted to destroy it by letting water from the moat reach the furnace – the resulting explosion caused the lean. Whatever the reason, the Marquess of Bute chose to leave the tower at a tilt when he restored the castle.

Canterbury Cathedral
Canterbury, Kent

1. Built: 1071-1498
2. Dedicated to: Christ
3. Architect: William of Sens/Henry Yevele
4. Height of tower: 235ft
5. Features: Medieval stained glass; modern windows by Erwin Bossanyi; Bell Harry Tower, named after the bell it houses
6. Other: Tombs of Thomas à Becket, Henry IV, the Black Prince; murder of Thomas à Becket, 1170; damaged during the Civil War; bombs fell in precinct during WWII

Tel: (01227) 762862

Canterbury Cathedral is the Mother Church of the Church of England and the seat of the Archbishop and Primate of All England, the Most Reverend and Right Honourable George L Carey PhD being the 103rd incumbent. Infamous for the murder there of Thomas à Becket in 1170, it was a fitting venue for the inaugural performance of TS Eliot's Murder in the Cathedral in 1935.

Cardiff Castle
Castle St, Cardiff

1. Inhabited
2. Built: 1093/19th century
3. Built for: Robert Fitzhamon, Lord of Gloucester
4. Features: Banqueting Hall and Gothick chapel
5. Other: Built on the site of a Roman fort, extensively modified by William Burges for 3rd Marquess of Bute, 19th century

Owner: City & County of Cardiff
Tel: (029) 2087 8100

The 3rd Marquess of Bute commissioned William Burges, as he did at Castell Coch, to undertake a complete overhaul of Cardiff Castle for him, spending a fortune on a castle he only lived in for six weeks a year.

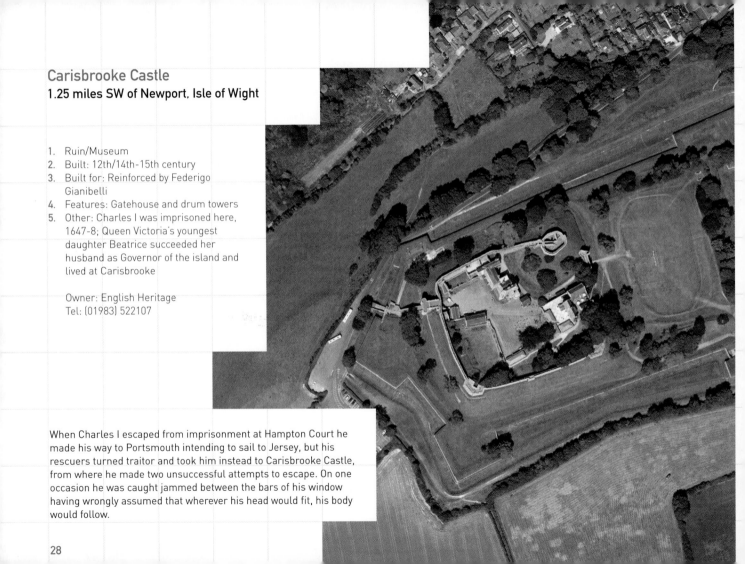

Carisbrooke Castle
1.25 miles SW of Newport, Isle of Wight

1. Ruin/Museum
2. Built: 12th/14th-15th century
3. Built for: Reinforced by Federigo Gianibelli
4. Features: Gatehouse and drum towers
5. Other: Charles I was imprisoned here, 1647-8; Queen Victoria's youngest daughter Beatrice succeeded her husband as Governor of the island and lived at Carisbrooke

Owner: English Heritage
Tel: (01983) 522107

When Charles I escaped from imprisonment at Hampton Court he made his way to Portsmouth intending to sail to Jersey, but his rescuers turned traitor and took him instead to Carisbrooke Castle, from where he made two unsuccessful attempts to escape. On one occasion he was caught jammed between the bars of his window having wrongly assumed that wherever his head would fit, his body would follow.

Castle Rising Castle
Castle Rising, Norfolk

1. Ruin
2. Built: 1140
3. Built for: William de Albini
4. Features: Vaulted ceilings and ornamented fireplaces survive
5. Other: William de Albini built the castle to celebrate his marriage to the widow of Henry I

Owner: Mr Greville Howard
Tel: (01553) 631330

Edward III banished his mother, Queen Isabella, to Castle Rising after she and her lover Roger Mortimer had imprisoned, tortured and murdered his father Edward II at Berkeley Castle. Isabella was described as the "she-wolf from France who tearest at the bowels of [her] mangled mate". Legend has it that she cut out Edward's heart and put it in a silver case, and that it was eventually buried with her at Greyfriars Monastery in London, where her ghost is said to haunt the churchyard.

Cawdor Castle
4.5 miles SW of Nairn, Speyside

1. Inhabited
2. Built: 14th-century keep
3. Family: Thanes of Cawdor
4. Features: Thorn Tree Room
5. Other: In Shakespeare's play the fulfilment of the witches' prophecy that Macbeth would become Thane of Cawdor sparks off his tragic pursuit of the crown

Owner: Campbells of Cawdor
Tel: (01667) 404615

Legend has it that a 14th-century Thane of Cawdor dreamt that he should build his castle on the spot where his donkey lay down to sleep. The next evening the donkey lay down by a thorn tree for shelter, and the building of Cawdor Castle began – today the Thorn Tree Room within the castle contains the remains of an ancient tree that have been carbon dated to 1372.

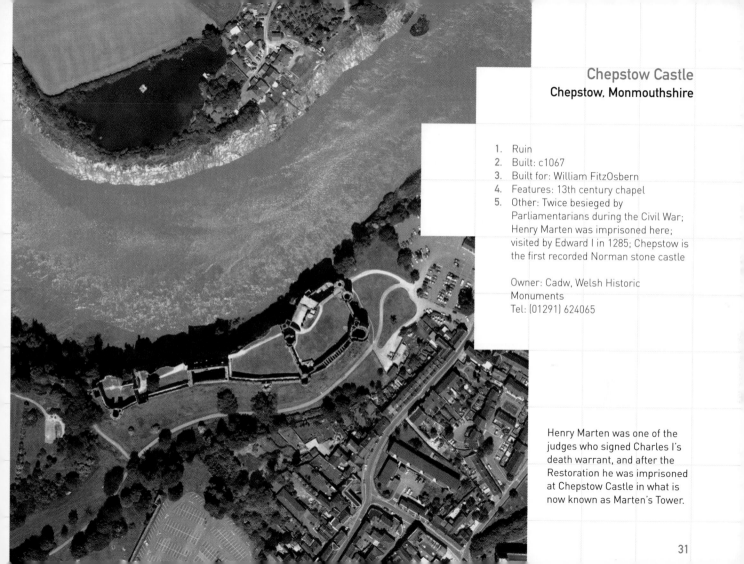

Chepstow Castle
Chepstow, Monmouthshire

1. Ruin
2. Built: c1067
3. Built for: William FitzOsbern
4. Features: 13th century chapel
5. Other: Twice besieged by Parliamentarians during the Civil War; Henry Marten was imprisoned here; visited by Edward I in 1285; Chepstow is the first recorded Norman stone castle

Owner: Cadw, Welsh Historic Monuments
Tel: (01291) 624065

Henry Marten was one of the judges who signed Charles I's death warrant, and after the Restoration he was imprisoned at Chepstow Castle in what is now known as Marten's Tower.

Chichester Cathedral
Chichester, West Sussex

1. Built: 1076-1108
2. Dedicated to: Holy Trinity
3. Architect: Bishop Ralph
4. Height of spire: 277ft
5. Features: Tapestries by John Piper and Ursula Benker-Schirmer; window by Marc Chagall; unique freestanding bell tower
6. Other: Tomb of Gustav Holst; Fitzalan tomb; paintings by Graham Sutherland, Hans Feibusch and Patrick Procktor, font by John Skelton and a sculpture of Christ in Judgement by Philip Jackson

Tel: (01243) 782595

Philip Larkin's poem An Arundel Tomb was inspired not by a tomb in Arundel Cathedral but by the 14th century Fitzalan tomb in Chichester Cathedral – the Fitzalans were Earls of Arundel for three hundred years. "Side by side, their faces blurred, the earl and countess lie in stone..." The poet notices that the stone effigies are holding hands and concludes, in one of Larkin's most famous lines, that they "prove our almost-instinct almost true: what will survive of us is love".

Conwy Castle
Conwy

1. Ruin
2. Built: 1283-88
3. Built for: Edward I
4. Features:15ft thick walls built in shape of Welsh harp
5. Other: Taken by cousins of Owain Glyndwr, 1401; taken by Major-General Mytton for Parliament, Civil War 1646; Richard II stayed, 1399 before being lured away and deposed by Bolingbroke (later Henry IV); although a ruin, the outer walls are almost intact; the three bridges alongside are the modern road bridge, Telford's Conwy Suspension Bridge (1817) and Stephenson's Tubular Bridge (1848)

Owner: Cadw, Welsh Historic Monuments
Tel: (01492) 592358

Conwy Castle took a mere five years to build – with 1500 men and a massive amount of public money. By 1609 the castle was described as "utterlie decayed", and in 1627 it was sold for just £100 to Charles I's Secretary of State, Lord Conway of Ragley. He persuaded the Archbishop of York, who was a Royalist and was born locally, to refortify the castle for the Civil War but it was nonetheless taken by Parliament and thereafter fell into decay.

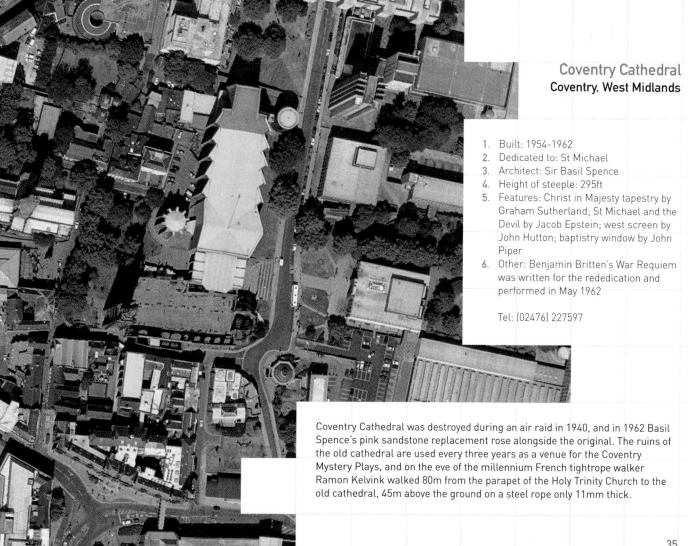

Coventry Cathedral
Coventry, West Midlands

1. Built: 1954-1962
2. Dedicated to: St Michael
3. Architect: Sir Basil Spence
4. Height of steeple: 295ft
5. Features: Christ in Majesty tapestry by Graham Sutherland; St Michael and the Devil by Jacob Epstein; west screen by John Hutton; baptistry window by John Piper
6. Other: Benjamin Britten's War Requiem was written for the rededication and performed in May 1962

Tel: (02476) 227597

Coventry Cathedral was destroyed during an air raid in 1940, and in 1962 Basil Spence's pink sandstone replacement rose alongside the original. The ruins of the old cathedral are used every three years as a venue for the Coventry Mystery Plays, and on the eve of the millennium French tightrope walker Ramon Kelvink walked 80m from the parapet of the Holy Trinity Church to the old cathedral, 45m above the ground on a steel rope only 11mm thick.

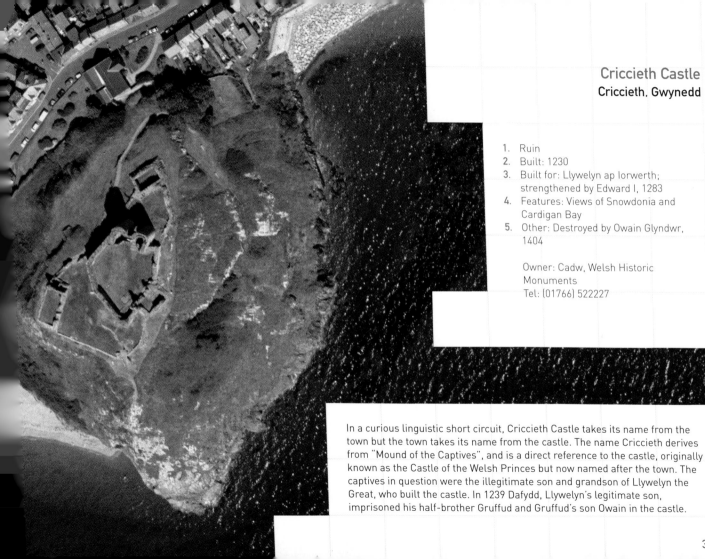

Criccieth Castle
Criccieth, Gwynedd

1. Ruin
2. Built: 1230
3. Built for: Llywelyn ap Iorwerth;
   strengthened by Edward I, 1283
4. Features: Views of Snowdonia and
   Cardigan Bay
5. Other: Destroyed by Owain Glyndwr,
   1404

Owner: Cadw, Welsh Historic
Monuments
Tel: (01766) 522227

In a curious linguistic short circuit, Criccieth Castle takes its name from the
town but the town takes its name from the castle. The name Criccieth derives
from "Mound of the Captives", and is a direct reference to the castle, originally
known as the Castle of the Welsh Princes but now named after the town. The
captives in question were the illegitimate son and grandson of Llywelyn the
Great, who built the castle. In 1239 Dafydd, Llywelyn's legitimate son,
imprisoned his half-brother Gruffud and Gruffud's son Owain in the castle.

Dartmouth Castle
1 mile SE of Dartmouth, Devon

1. Restored
2. Built: 1481
3. Built for: the merchants of Dartmouth
4. Features: The first castle in England designed specifically to withstand artillery
5. Other: Never saw military action; faces Kingswear Castle across the Dart estuary; a chain could be drawn between the two in times of war

Owner: English Heritage
Tel: (01803) 833588

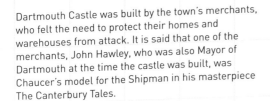

Dartmouth Castle was built by the town's merchants, who felt the need to protect their homes and warehouses from attack. It is said that one of the merchants, John Hawley, who was also Mayor of Dartmouth at the time the castle was built, was Chaucer's model for the Shipman in his masterpiece The Canterbury Tales.

Deal Castle
Deal, Kent

1. Uninhabited
2. Built: 1539-40
3. Built for: Henry VIII
4. Features: The plan of the castle is the shape of a Tudor rose
5. Other: Deal defends the stretch of coast that centuries earlier was the site of Julius Caesar's first successful landing

Owner: English Heritage
Tel: (01304) 372762

Henry VIII's break with the Roman church brought fears that Roman Catholic forces in Europe might invade Britain, so some twenty forts were built along the south coast. Five castles were quickly built close to Deal, of which Deal itself was the most powerful, but modern commentator Christina Gascoigne questions their pedigree as castles, saying that they are "more akin to elaborate Martello Towers than to true castles".

Dean Castle
Kilmarnock

1. Uninhabited
2. Built: 14th/15th century
3. Family: Balliol/Boyd
4. Features: Collection of medieval arms and armour; display of Burns' manuscripts
5. Other: The lands were given to the Boyd family by Robert the Bruce; the castle was gutted by fire in 1735 and abandoned but restored from 1905 using stone from Balconie castle

Owner: East Ayrshire council
Tel: (01563) 522702

Donated to the town of Kilmarnock in 1975, Dean Castle, once known as Kilmarnock Castle, now houses a museum. It is set in a wooded country park with rivers, gardens, woodlands and an adventure playground.

Derby Cathedral
Derby, Derbyshire

1. Built: 16th century/1725/1972
2. Dedicated to: All Saints
3. Architect: restored by James Gibbs
4. Height of west tower: 212ft
5. Features: 18th century wrought iron screen by Robert Bakewell
6. Other: Tomb of Henry Cavendish, who discovered hydrogen; monument to Bess of Hardwick; the parish church of All Saints became a cathedral in 1927

Tel: (01332) 341201

Derby Cathedral was restored during the 18th century by the distinguished Scottish architect James Gibbs, who is described as "the most influential London church architect of the early 18th century". He went to Rome in 1703 to train for the priesthood but gave that up after a year and studied painting before turning to architecture. His first building was St Mary-le-Strand in London and his most radical building the Radcliffe Library in Oxford, aka the Radcliffe Camera, but without doubt his masterpiece is the London church of St Martin-in-the-Fields.

Dover Castle
Dover, Kent

1. Uninhabited
2. Built: 1168-88
3. Built for: Henry II
4. Features: Roman lighthouse; Napoleonic tunnel systems used as base for the evacuation of Dunkirk
5. Other: Successfully besieged by Louis of France in 1216; taken by Parliamentarians, Civil War 1642; Edward I was imprisoned here before his accession; known as The Key of England because of its strategic importance

Owner: English Heritage
Tel: (01304) 211067

William the Conqueror considered Dover Castle to be so important that he placed it in the charge of his half-brother, Bishop Odo of Bayeaux. Since then constables in charge have included Henry V, Henry VIII, James II and George V prior to their accession, William Pitt, the Duke of Wellington, Lord Palmerston and Sir Winston Churchill.

Dunstanburgh Castle
Embleton, Northumberland

1. Ruin
2. Built: 1313-16
3. Built for: Earl of Lancaster; enlarged by John of Gaunt
4. Features: Stands on cliffs rising 100ft above the North Sea
5. Other: Lancastrian stronghold during the Wars of the Roses; forced to surrender during the Civil War 1462 and 1464; inspired many paintings, including three Turners

Owner: English Heritage
Tel: (01665) 576231

Thomas, Earl of Lancaster, the builder of Dunstanburgh Castle, was the leader of the baronial opposition to Edward II and probably intended the castle as a place of refuge in case of the failure of his cause. Already protected by the sea to the north and east, it was further strengthened by John of Gaunt, Duke of Lancaster, when he converted the gatehouse into a keep.

Durham Cathedral
Durham, County Durham

1. Built: 1093-1140/later additions
2. Dedicated to: Christ & St Mary
3. Architect: William of St Carileph
4. Height of tower: 218ft
5. Features: 12th-century sanctuary knocker; the first pointed arches and ribbed vaulting in Europe
6. Other: Tombs of St Cuthbert and the Venerable Bede; the Puritans held Scottish prisoners here during the Civil War; stands on a 70ft rock surrounded on three sides by the River Wear

Tel: (0191) 386 4266

The 12th century brass sanctuary knocker at Durham is a reminder of the medieval distinction between secular and religious law. Lawbreakers who reached a circle of wooden crosses around the church could claim sanctuary from the lay authorities for up to 35 days; after this time, the monks would usually give them a robe of St Cuthbert and a wooden cross, which gave them the protection of the church until they reached the nearest port.

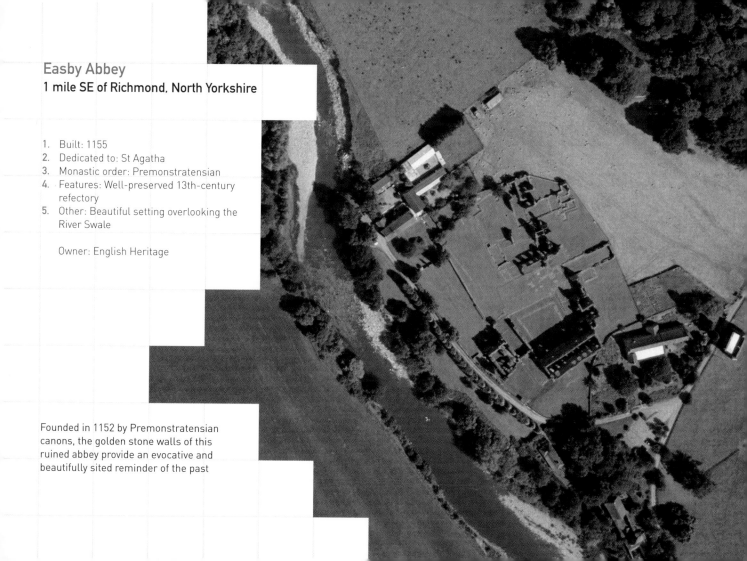

Easby Abbey
1 mile SE of Richmond, North Yorkshire

1. Built: 1155
2. Dedicated to: St Agatha
3. Monastic order: Premonstratensian
4. Features: Well-preserved 13th-century refectory
5. Other: Beautiful setting overlooking the River Swale

   Owner: English Heritage

Founded in 1152 by Premonstratensian canons, the golden stone walls of this ruined abbey provide an evocative and beautifully sited reminder of the past

Edinburgh Castle
Edinburgh, Midlothian

1. Inhabited
2. Built: 11th century onwards
3. Built for: Scottish royalty
4. Features: Honours of Scotland (Scottish Crown Jewels), Scottish National War Memorial, Stone of Destiny (aka Stone of Scone)
5. Other: Taken by the English in 1174 for a short time, and again in 1296 until it was recaptured by the Earl of Moray 16 years later. Slighted by Robert the Bruce, refortified by the English then retaken by the Scots in 1341. Surrendered to Cromwell in 1650 after a three month siege. Held for James VII of Scotland, II of England, in 1689 against William of Orange; legend has it that the infant James I was lowered from the castle walls in a basket to be secretly baptised into the Old Faith; the strategic importance of the castle led to the emergence of Edinburgh as the capital of Scotland

Owner: Historic Scotland
Tel: (0131) 225 9846

There is an apocryphal story that one tourist, looking over the fortifications towards Prince's Street Gardens, was heard to ask why Edinburgh Castle had been built so close to the railway. The castle is the home of the Honours of Scotland, which were last used in 1651 for the Scottish coronation of Charles II, nine years before the Restoration and ten before his coronation as King of England. Cromwell was so enraged by the coronation that he made exhaustive attempts to seize the Honours and have them melted down. Much to the annoyance of the people of Perth and the curators of Scone Palace, Edinburgh Castle has also been the home of the Stone of Destiny since its return to Scotland from Westminster Abbey.

Ely Cathedral
Ely, Cambridgeshire

1. Built: c1081-1189
2. Dedicated to: Holy Trinity
3. Architect: Abbot Simeon/restored by Scott
4. Height of west tower 215ft
5. Features: Alan de Walsingham's Octagon Tower, unique in England
6. Other: The name Ely comes from Eel Island, from the Saxon staple diet

Tel: (01353) 667735

The cathedral stands on the site of a monastery founded by St Etheldreda, who, despite being twice married, is honoured as a virgin. St Etheldreda was also known as St Awdrey – an annual fair was held on her feast day at which cheap trinkets were sold, the quality of the goods on sale at St Awdrey's Fair being the origin of the word tawdry.

Exeter Cathedral
Exeter, Devon

1. Built: 1112-36/c1270-1350
2. Dedicated to: St Peter
3. Architect: Bishop Warelwast/restored by Scott
4. Height of towers: 130ft
5. Features: Old English Exeter Book; Exon Domesday; 59ft high Bishop's throne; astronomical clock; Great Peter bell in the North Tower
6. Other: Monument to Hugh de Courteney; damaged by air raids during WWII; the west front has 68 statues including kings Alfred the Great, Athelstan, Canute, Edward the Confessor, William the Conqueror and Richard II

Tel: (01392) 055573

Professor Freeman writes that Exeter Cathedral "exhibits perhaps the most perfect specimen of bilateral symmetry. Not only does aisle answer to aisle, and pillar to pillar, and window tracery to window tracery, but also chapel to chapel, screen to screen, and even tomb to tomb, and canopy to canopy".

Fort George
11 miles NE of Inverness, Highland

1. Inhabited
2. Built: 1747-69
3. Built for: Crown
4. Features: Houses the regimental museum of The Queen's Own Highlanders; built on sandy spit jutting into Moray Firth
5. Other: Considered by military architectural historians to be one of the finest fortifications in Europe

Owner: Historic Scotland
Tel: (01667) 462800

This polygonal fort, vaguely reminiscent of the Pentagon, was built as a base for George II's army to suppress any attempt to resurrect the Jacobite cause. By the time Fort George was completed the uprising had already been quashed, and the fort has been used ever since as a military barracks.

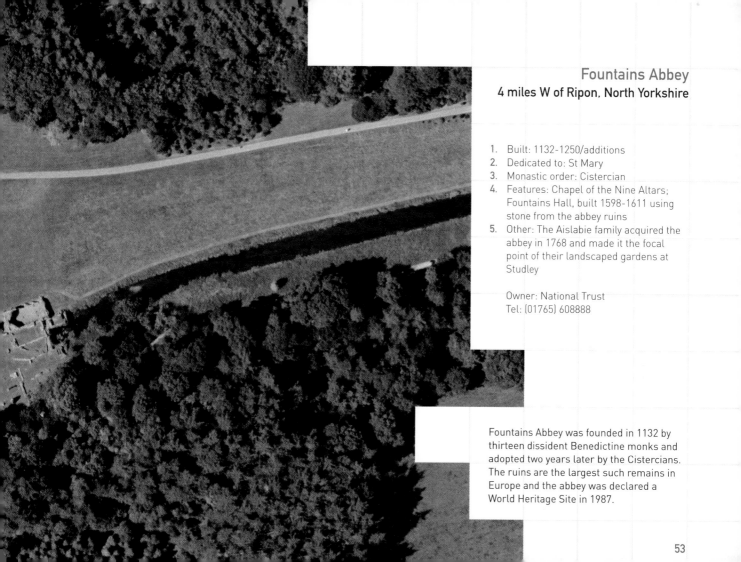

Fountains Abbey
4 miles W of Ripon, North Yorkshire

1. Built: 1132-1250/additions
2. Dedicated to: St Mary
3. Monastic order: Cistercian
4. Features: Chapel of the Nine Altars; Fountains Hall, built 1598-1611 using stone from the abbey ruins
5. Other: The Aislabie family acquired the abbey in 1768 and made it the focal point of their landscaped gardens at Studley

Owner: National Trust
Tel: (01765) 608888

Fountains Abbey was founded in 1132 by thirteen dissident Benedictine monks and adopted two years later by the Cistercians. The ruins are the largest such remains in Europe and the abbey was declared a World Heritage Site in 1987.

Framlingham Castle
Framlingham, Suffolk

1. Partially restored
2. Built: 1177-1215
3. Built for: Roger Bigod
4. Features: No keep; 13 towers and curtain walls
5. Other: Besieged and captured by King John, 1219; King John stayed as guest of Bigod, 1213; Princess Mary stayed in 1553 and the Earl of Arundel brought the news that she was Queen

Owner: English Heritage
Tel: (01728) 724189

Henry III paid a group of stonemasons and carpenters £14.15s.11d. to have Framlingham Castle demolished but it seems that the builders did not fulfill their contract and Roger Bigod was able to rebuild it. The castle played no part in the Civil War but was partially demolished during the 17th century when it was bequeathed to Pembroke College, Cambridge, on condition that "all the Castle, saving the stone building, be pulled down" to make way for a poorhouse to be built within the castle walls.

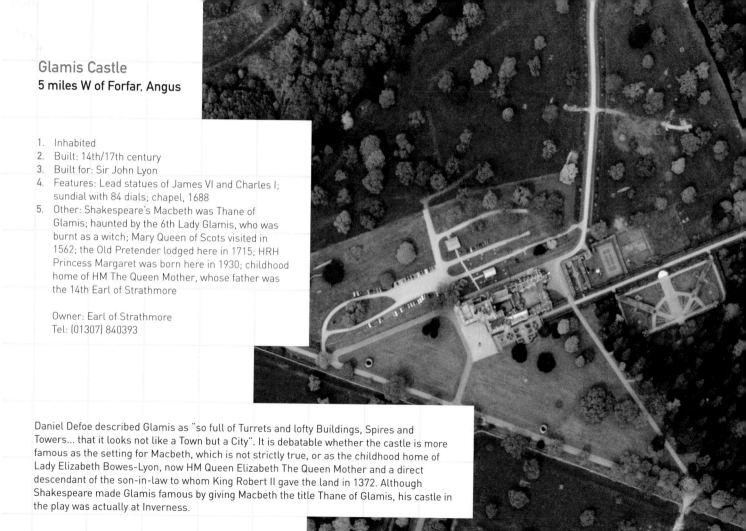

Glamis Castle
5 miles W of Forfar, Angus

1. Inhabited
2. Built: 14th/17th century
3. Built for: Sir John Lyon
4. Features: Lead statues of James VI and Charles I;
   sundial with 84 dials; chapel, 1688
5. Other: Shakespeare's Macbeth was Thane of
   Glamis; haunted by the 6th Lady Glamis, who was
   burnt as a witch; Mary Queen of Scots visited in
   1562; the Old Pretender lodged here in 1715; HRH
   Princess Margaret was born here in 1930; childhood
   home of HM The Queen Mother, whose father was
   the 14th Earl of Strathmore

Owner: Earl of Strathmore
Tel: (01307) 840393

Daniel Defoe described Glamis as "so full of Turrets and lofty Buildings, Spires and Towers... that it looks not like a Town but a City". It is debatable whether the castle is more famous as the setting for Macbeth, which is not strictly true, or as the childhood home of Lady Elizabeth Bowes-Lyon, now HM Queen Elizabeth The Queen Mother and a direct descendant of the son-in-law to whom King Robert II gave the land in 1372. Although Shakespeare made Glamis famous by giving Macbeth the title Thane of Glamis, his castle in the play was actually at Inverness.

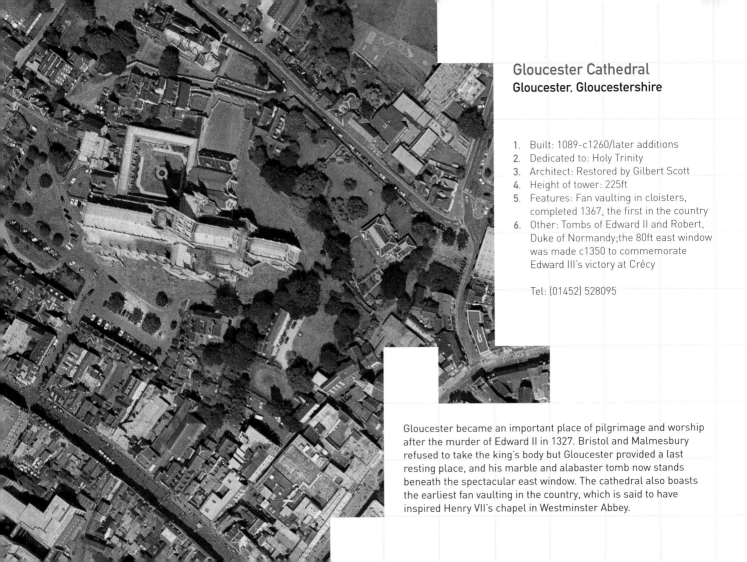

Gloucester Cathedral
Gloucester, Gloucestershire

1. Built: 1089–c1260/later additions
2. Dedicated to: Holy Trinity
3. Architect: Restored by Gilbert Scott
4. Height of tower: 225ft
5. Features: Fan vaulting in cloisters, completed 1367, the first in the country
6. Other: Tombs of Edward II and Robert, Duke of Normandy;the 80ft east window was made c1350 to commemorate Edward III's victory at Crécy

Tel: (01452) 528095

Gloucester became an important place of pilgrimage and worship after the murder of Edward II in 1327. Bristol and Malmesbury refused to take the king's body but Gloucester provided a last resting place, and his marble and alabaster tomb now stands beneath the spectacular east window. The cathedral also boasts the earliest fan vaulting in the country, which is said to have inspired Henry VII's chapel in Westminster Abbey.

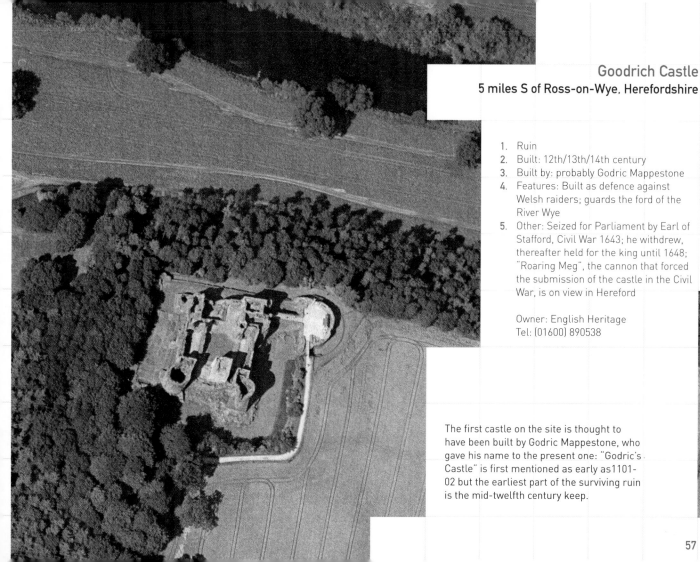

Goodrich Castle
5 miles S of Ross-on-Wye, Herefordshire

1. Ruin
2. Built: 12th/13th/14th century
3. Built by: probably Godric Mappestone
4. Features: Built as defence against Welsh raiders; guards the ford of the River Wye
5. Other: Seized for Parliament by Earl of Stafford, Civil War 1643; he withdrew, thereafter held for the king until 1648; "Roaring Meg", the cannon that forced the submission of the castle in the Civil War, is on view in Hereford

Owner: English Heritage
Tel: (01600) 890538

The first castle on the site is thought to have been built by Godric Mappestone, who gave his name to the present one: "Godric's Castle" is first mentioned as early as 1101-02 but the earliest part of the surviving ruin is the mid-twelfth century keep.

Guildford Cathedral
Guildford, Surrey

1. Built: 1936-65
2. Dedicated to: Holy Spirit
3. Architect: Sir Edward Maufe
4. Height of central tower: 160ft
5. Features: Used as a location for the film The Omen
6. Other: Dedicated May 1961

Tel: (01483) 565287

Guildford Cathedral, towering above the A3 on Stag Hill, has been described as looking from the outside like an oversized crematorium, with an interior that "has all the spirituality of a concert hall, but without the acoustics".

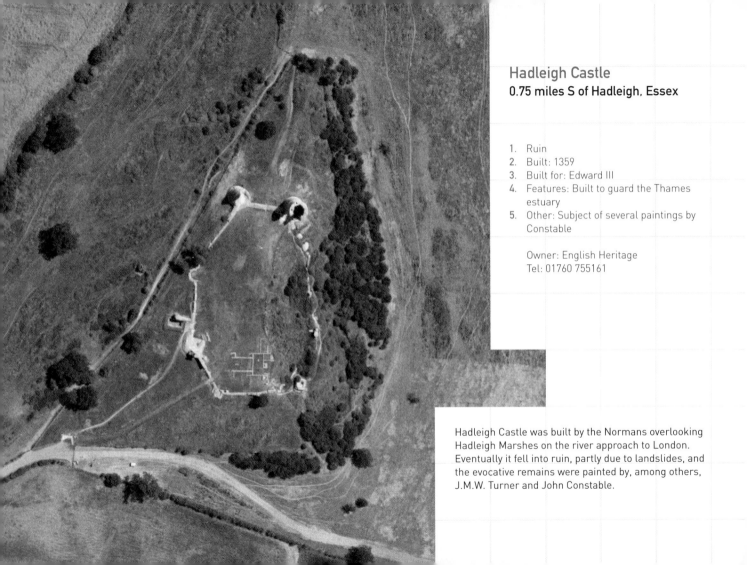

Hadleigh Castle
0.75 miles S of Hadleigh, Essex

1. Ruin
2. Built: 1359
3. Built for: Edward III
4. Features: Built to guard the Thames estuary
5. Other: Subject of several paintings by Constable

Owner: English Heritage
Tel: 01760 755161

Hadleigh Castle was built by the Normans overlooking Hadleigh Marshes on the river approach to London. Eventually it fell into ruin, partly due to landslides, and the evocative remains were painted by, among others, J.M.W. Turner and John Constable.

Harlech Castle
Harlech, Gwynedd

1. Ruin
2. Built: c1283-91
3. Built for: Edward I
4. Features: Built on a 200ft bluff, the site of an early Celtic fortress
5. Other: Taken by Owain Glyndwr 1404; taken back 1409; besieged for seven years by Yorkists during the Wars of the Roses, ending 1468; taken by Parliament 1647 during Civil War; the defence of the castle by Dafydd ap Einion during the Wars of the Roses inspired the song "Men of Harlech"

Owner: Cadw, Welsh Historic Monuments
Tel: (01766) 780552

The sea once washed against the spectacular rock on which Harlech Castle was built but it has since receded. The problem with being accessible from only one direction was that besiegers could fairly easily cut off supplies to the castle, which may account for the large number of times it changed hands, but its superb defences meant that it was the last North Wales stronghold to fall to the Yorkists in the Wars of the Roses, and the last to fall to Parliament in the Civil War.

Hedingham Castle
Castle Hedingham, Essex

1. In use
2. Built: 1140
3. Family: de Vere, Earls of Oxford
4. Features: Norman keep 100ft high
5. Other: Besieged by King John; visited by
   Henry VII, Henry VIII and Elizabeth I

Owner: The Hon Thomas Lindsay
Tel: (01787) 460261

Hedingham Castle is one of the best preserved Norman keeps in
England, built by the famous medieval family the de Veres, Earls of
Oxford, and still owned by their descendants. The huge Norman
keep includes a magnificent Banqueting Hall and Minstrels' Gallery
and is approached by a Tudor bridge that was built in 1496 to
replace the drawbridge.

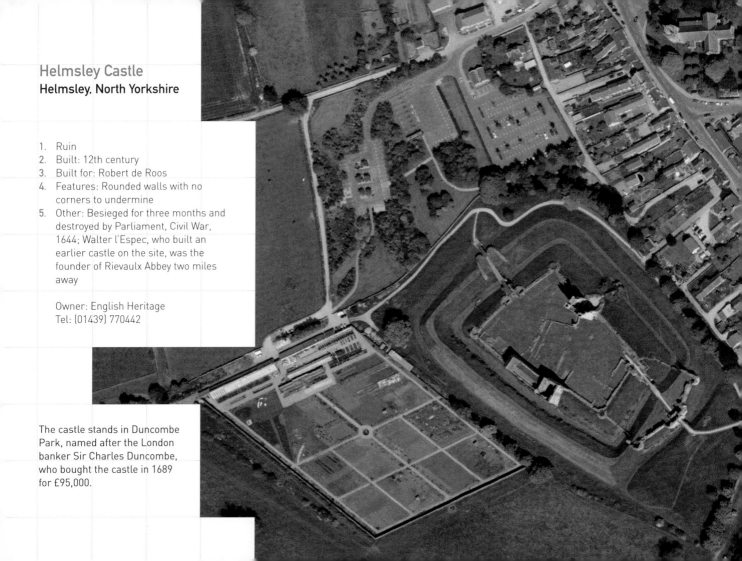

Helmsley Castle
Helmsley, North Yorkshire

1. Ruin
2. Built: 12th century
3. Built for: Robert de Roos
4. Features: Rounded walls with no corners to undermine
5. Other: Besieged for three months and destroyed by Parliament, Civil War, 1644; Walter l'Espec, who built an earlier castle on the site, was the founder of Rievaulx Abbey two miles away

Owner: English Heritage
Tel: (01439) 770442

The castle stands in Duncombe Park, named after the London banker Sir Charles Duncombe, who bought the castle in 1689 for £95,000.

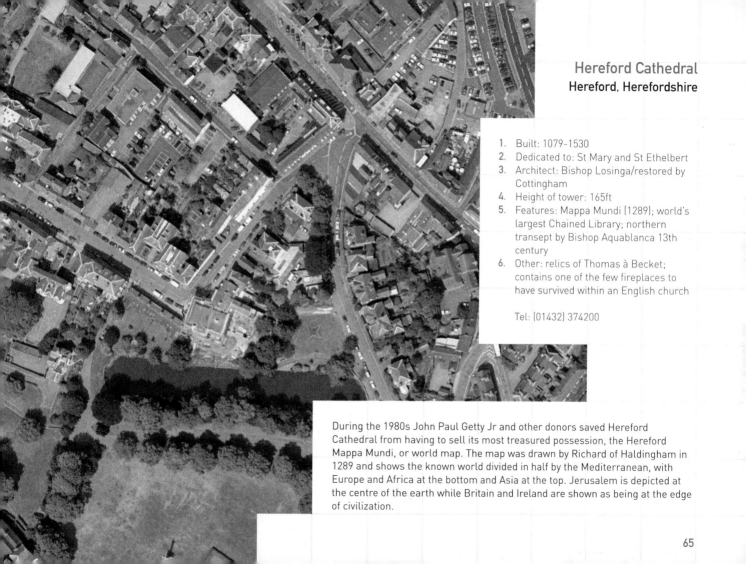

Hereford Cathedral
Hereford. Herefordshire

1. Built: 1079-1530
2. Dedicated to: St Mary and St Ethelbert
3. Architect: Bishop Losinga/restored by Cottingham
4. Height of tower: 165ft
5. Features: Mappa Mundi (1289); world's largest Chained Library; northern transept by Bishop Aquablanca 13th century
6. Other: relics of Thomas à Becket; contains one of the few fireplaces to have survived within an English church

Tel: (01432) 374200

During the 1980s John Paul Getty Jr and other donors saved Hereford Cathedral from having to sell its most treasured possession, the Hereford Mappa Mundi, or world map. The map was drawn by Richard of Haldingham in 1289 and shows the known world divided in half by the Mediterranean, with Europe and Africa at the bottom and Asia at the top. Jerusalem is depicted at the centre of the earth while Britain and Ireland are shown as being at the edge of civilization.

Herstmonceux Castle
Hailsham, East Sussex

1. Restored
2. Built: 1441/20th century
3. Built for: Roger de Fiennes
4. Features: Gatehouse towers 84ft high
5. Other: Saw almost no military action; in the 1770s the owner, the Rev Robert Hare, dismantled the castle to build himself a new house but it was later restored by a subsequent owner, Sir Claude Lowther, whose work was completed by his successor Sir Paul Latham.

Owner: Queen's University, Ontario, Canada
Tel: (01323) 833816

Sir Roger de Fiennes would probably have approved of the 20th century restoration of his striking Flemish brick castle, but he would have been surprised and confused by the sight of the domes that appeared when the Royal Observatory moved from Greenwich to Herstmonceaux in search of cleaner air. The castle is currently owned by a Canadian university and used as an international study centre.

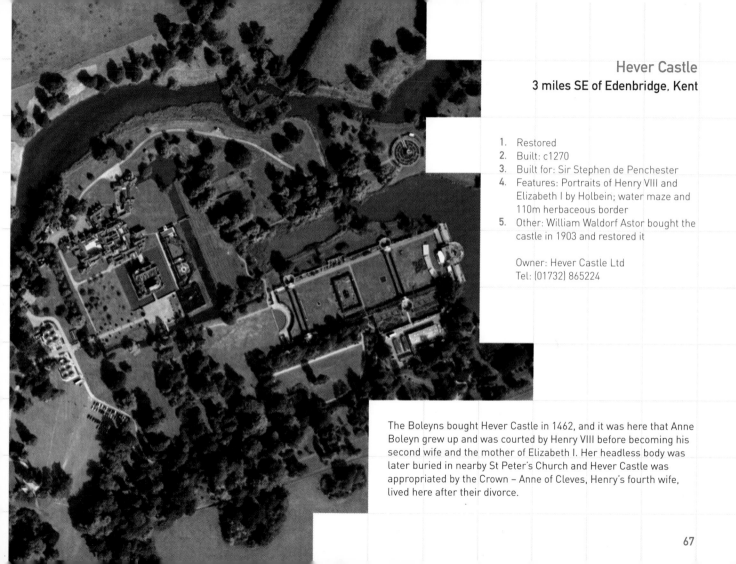

Hever Castle
3 miles SE of Edenbridge, Kent

1. Restored
2. Built: c1270
3. Built for: Sir Stephen de Penchester
4. Features: Portraits of Henry VIII and Elizabeth I by Holbein; water maze and 110m herbaceous border
5. Other: William Waldorf Astor bought the castle in 1903 and restored it

Owner: Hever Castle Ltd
Tel: (01732) 865224

The Boleyns bought Hever Castle in 1462, and it was here that Anne Boleyn grew up and was courted by Henry VIII before becoming his second wife and the mother of Elizabeth I. Her headless body was later buried in nearby St Peter's Church and Hever Castle was appropriated by the Crown – Anne of Cleves, Henry's fourth wife, lived here after their divorce.

Kenilworth Castle
Kenilworth, Warwickshire

1. Ruin
2. Built: 12th/14th century
3. Family: de Montfort/Gaunt/Dudley
4. Features: Gaunt's banqueting hall
5. Other: Changed hands during the Civil
   War with little fighting; slighted 1649;
   setting for Sir Walter Scott's novel
   Kenilworth; appears in Marlowe's
   Edward II; Princes Edward and Richard,
   sons of Henry III, were imprisoned here;
   Edward II signed his abdication here;
   transformed by John of Gaunt and used
   as a royal residence from the time of
   Henry IV until Elizabeth I gave it to
   Robert Dudley

Owner: English Heritage
Tel: (01926) 852078

Kenilworth is most famous for the siege of 1266 when Henry III and
Prince Edward (later Edward I) defeated Simon de Montfort the
younger, and for the lavish entertainment provided here by Robert
Dudley, Earl of Leicester, for Elizabeth I. Dudley built a new wing to
accommodate the queen, and the entertainment, recorded as "The
Princeley Pleasures of the Castle of Kenelwoorthe", lasted 19 days
at a cost to Dudley of £1000 a day.

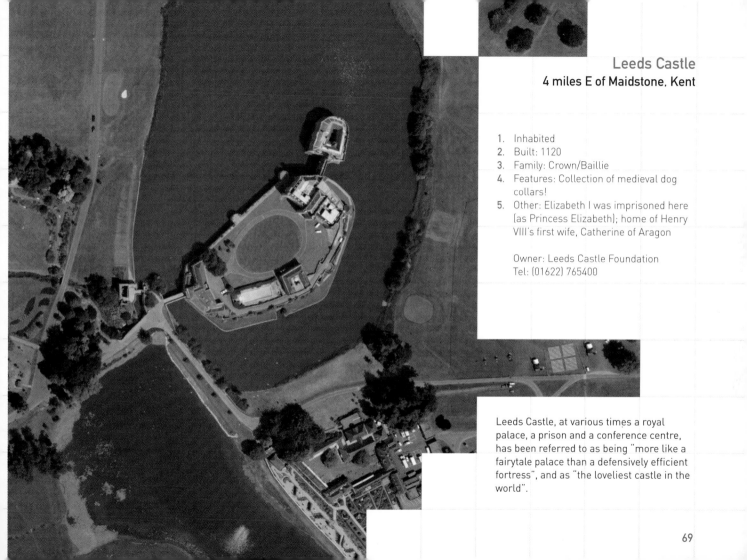

Leeds Castle
4 miles E of Maidstone, Kent

1. Inhabited
2. Built: 1120
3. Family: Crown/Baillie
4. Features: Collection of medieval dog collars!
5. Other: Elizabeth I was imprisoned here (as Princess Elizabeth); home of Henry VIII's first wife, Catherine of Aragon

Owner: Leeds Castle Foundation
Tel: (01622) 765400

Leeds Castle, at various times a royal palace, a prison and a conference centre, has been referred to as being "more like a fairytale palace than a defensively efficient fortress", and as "the loveliest castle in the world".

Lichfield Cathedral
Lichfield, Staffordshire

1. Built: 1195-14th century
2. Dedicated to: St Mary and St Chad
3. Architect: Restored by Gilbert Scott
4. Height of spire: 258ft
5. Features: Lichfield Gospels (8th century), sculptures by Chantry and Epstein; 16th-century windows in the Lady Chapel brought from Herkenrode Abbey in Belgium
6. Other: Bust of Samuel Johnson; the cathedral is unique in having three spires, known as "The Ladies of the Vale"

Tel: (01543) 306240

Lichfield Cathedral was more damaged than any other by Cromwell's troops during the Civil War. They shot away the central spire, stripped lead from the roofs and smashed much of the stained glass. They also destroyed images, monuments, and most of the 13th century statues that adorned the West Front of the cathedral. Today there are more than one hundred statues of Biblical and historical figures, most of them 19th century replacements for the ones smashed by the Parliamentarians.

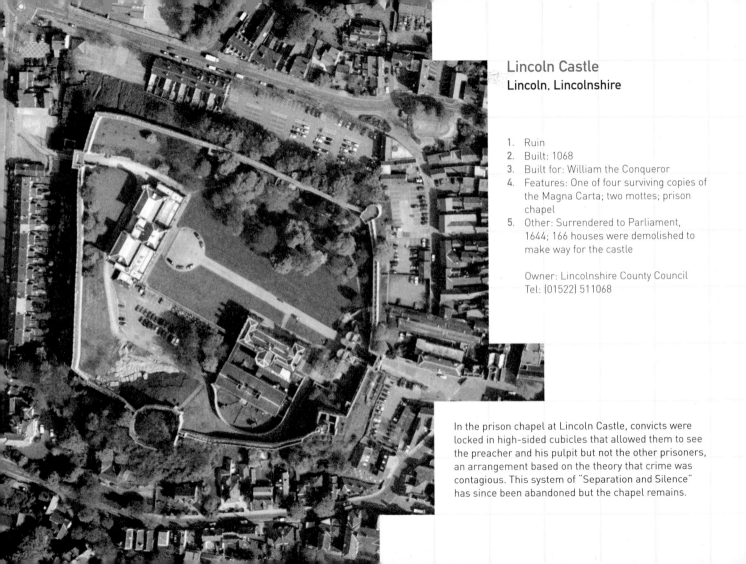

Lincoln Castle
Lincoln, Lincolnshire

1. Ruin
2. Built: 1068
3. Built for: William the Conqueror
4. Features: One of four surviving copies of the Magna Carta; two mottes; prison chapel
5. Other: Surrendered to Parliament, 1644; 166 houses were demolished to make way for the castle

Owner: Lincolnshire County Council
Tel: (01522) 511068

In the prison chapel at Lincoln Castle, convicts were locked in high-sided cubicles that allowed them to see the preacher and his pulpit but not the other prisoners, an arrangement based on the theory that crime was contagious. This system of "Separation and Silence" has since been abandoned but the chapel remains.

Lincoln Cathedral
Lincoln, Lincolnshire

1. Built: 1074-14th century/20th century
2. Dedicated to: St Mary
3. Architect: Bishop Hugh/restored by RS Godfrey
4. Height of tower: 271ft
5. Features: 5 ton bell "Great Tom of Lincoln"; copy of Magna Carta; St Hugh's choir; the Angel Choir; Wren library
6. Other: Tomb of Robert Grosseteste; early parliament met here (1301); famous for the tiny Lincoln Imp

Tel: (01522) 544544

The cathedral has been largely rebuilt twice, after a fire in 1141 and an earthquake in 1185. John Ruskin wrote of it that "I have always held and am prepared against all evidence to maintain that the Cathedral of Lincoln is out and out the most precious piece of architecture in the British Isles and roughly speaking worth any two other cathedrals we have."

Liverpool Cathedral
Liverpool, Merseyside

1. Built: 1904-78
2. Dedicated to: Christ
3. Architect: Sir Giles Gilbert Scott
4. Height of tower: 331ft
5. Features: Reredos over 50ft high; Vestey Tower
6. Other: Damaged by WWII bombs; brown-red sandstone quarried at Woolton, within the city boundaries

Tel: (0151) 709 6271

Liverpool's Anglican cathedral looks much more ancient than the city's Roman Catholic cathedral but in fact it was completed eleven years later. It is Britain's largest cathedral, the world's fifth largest, and has the world's tallest Gothic arches, the largest (though not the tallest) tower in the world and the highest and heaviest bells.

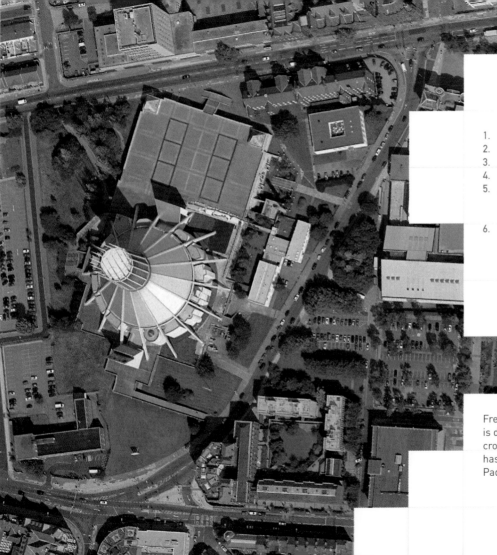

Liverpool RC Cathedral
Liverpool, Merseyside

1. Built: 1952-67
2. Dedicated to: Christ the King
3. Architect: Frederick Gibberd
4. Height: 290ft
5. Features: Glass by John Piper and Patrick Reyntiens; sixteen-sided lantern tower with tapering walls
6. Other: Originally designed by Lutyens as a Classical cathedral but the war and costs forced a change of plan

Tel: (0151) 709 9222

Frederick Gibberd's conical lantern tower is described by its supporters in terms of crowns and coronas, but its unusual shape has also led to the cathedral being called Paddy's Wigwam and the Mersey Funnel.

Loudoun Castle
Galston, Ayrshire

1. Ruin
2. Built: 15th century/1804-11
3. Built for: Flora Mure-Campbell (19th century)
4. Features: 500 acre theme park
5. Other: Haunted by the Grey Lady, a phantom piper and a monk who says pax vobiscum (peace be with you); destroyed by fire, 1st December 1941; in its heyday the massive castle had over ninety apartments and was known as The Windsor of Scotland

Owner: Raymond Codona
Tel: (01563) 822296

Sir Hugh de Crawford (or Craufurd) of Loudoun was the grandfather of Sir William Wallace (1273 - 1305), the great Scottish patriot who was born nearby at Ellerslie outside Kilmarnock. One of Wallace's swords once hung in Loudoun Castle but was sold by auction in 1930.

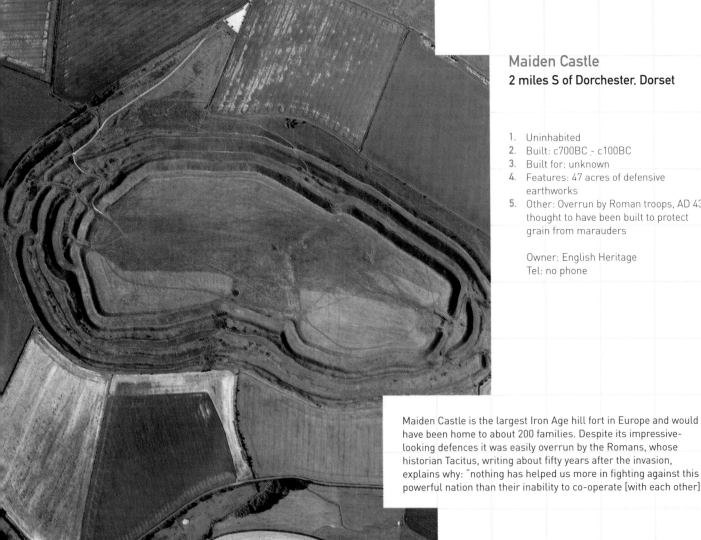

Maiden Castle
2 miles S of Dorchester, Dorset

1. Uninhabited
2. Built: c700BC - c100BC
3. Built for: unknown
4. Features: 47 acres of defensive earthworks
5. Other: Overrun by Roman troops, AD 43; thought to have been built to protect grain from marauders

   Owner: English Heritage
   Tel: no phone

Maiden Castle is the largest Iron Age hill fort in Europe and would have been home to about 200 families. Despite its impressive-looking defences it was easily overrun by the Romans, whose historian Tacitus, writing about fifty years after the invasion, explains why: "nothing has helped us more in fighting against this powerful nation than their inability to co-operate [with each other]".

Newcastle Cathedral
Newcastle, Tyne & Wear

1. Built: 14th/15th century
2. Dedicated to: St Nicholas
3. Architect: Additions by RJ Johnson
4. Height of spire: 194ft
5. Features: Pre-Reformation font and lectern; Hexham Bible, c1220; pinnacled lantern tower; earliest and best example in Britain of a "crown spire"
6. Other: Raised to cathedral status 1882; England's most northerly cathedral

Tel: (0191) 232 1939

Newcastle Cathedral contains one of the largest funerary brasses in England, commissioned by Roger Thornton, Newcastle's very own Dick Whittington, who arrived in the city penniless but died its richest merchant.

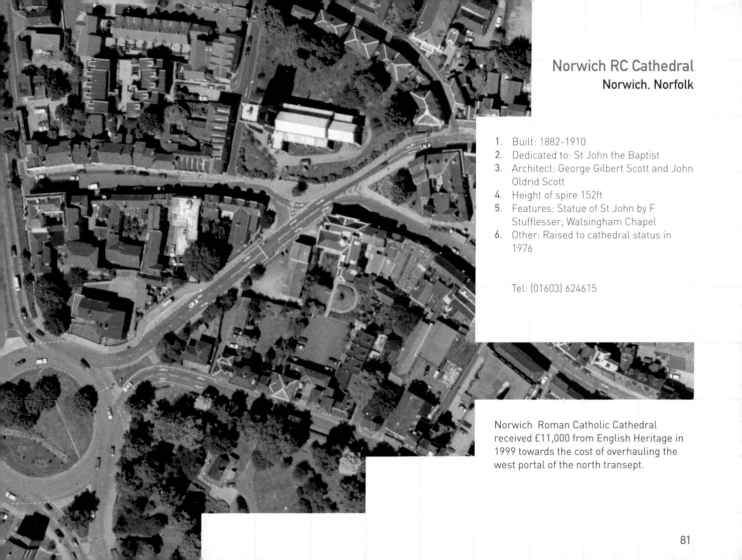

Norwich RC Cathedral
Norwich, Norfolk

1. Built: 1882-1910
2. Dedicated to: St John the Baptist
3. Architect: George Gilbert Scott and John Oldrid Scott
4. Height of spire 152ft
5. Features: Statue of St John by F Stufflesser; Walsingham Chapel
6. Other: Raised to cathedral status in 1976

Tel: (01603) 624615

Norwich Roman Catholic Cathedral received £11,000 from English Heritage in 1999 towards the cost of overhauling the west portal of the north transept.

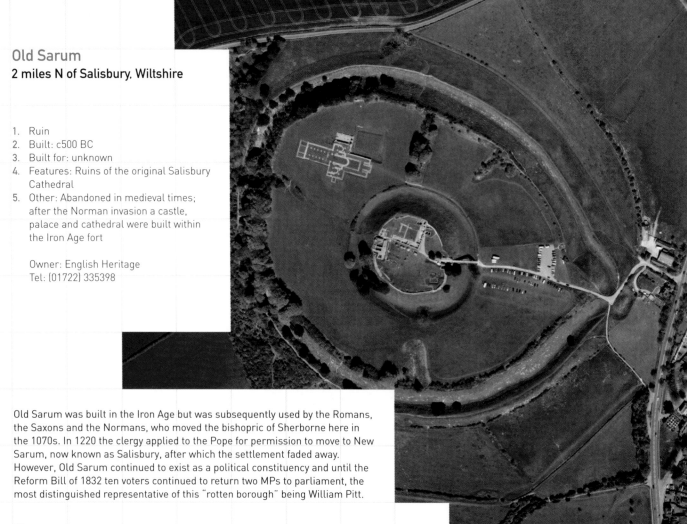

Old Sarum
2 miles N of Salisbury, Wiltshire

1. Ruin
2. Built: c500 BC
3. Built for: unknown
4. Features: Ruins of the original Salisbury Cathedral
5. Other: Abandoned in medieval times; after the Norman invasion a castle, palace and cathedral were built within the Iron Age fort

   Owner: English Heritage
   Tel: (01722) 335398

Old Sarum was built in the Iron Age but was subsequently used by the Romans, the Saxons and the Normans, who moved the bishopric of Sherborne here in the 1070s. In 1220 the clergy applied to the Pope for permission to move to New Sarum, now known as Salisbury, after which the settlement faded away. However, Old Sarum continued to exist as a political constituency and until the Reform Bill of 1832 ten voters continued to return two MPs to parliament, the most distinguished representative of this "rotten borough" being William Pitt.

Orford Castle
Orford, Suffolk

1. Ruin
2. Built: 1165-73
3. Built for: Henry II
4. Features: Unique eighteen-sided keep
5. Other: Taken by French Prince Louis after King John's death; taken and retaken during reign of Henry III; built between Framlingham Castle and the sea in order to subdue Hugh Bigod - King Henry later ordered the dismantling of Framlingham

Owner: English Heritage
Tel: (01394) 450472

The town of Orford was once a busy port on the River Alde, and legend has it that during the 12th century a naked merman was brought to the castle's first constable. However, the story could never be substantiated because the merman "secretly fled to the sea and was never afterwards seen".

Oxford Cathedral
Oxford, Oxfordshire

1. Built: 1158-1250
2. Dedicated to: Christ
3. Architect: Restored by Gilbert Scott
4. Height of spire: 144ft
5. Features: Stained glass by Edward Burne-Jones
6. Other: Tomb of George Berkeley; shrine of St Frideswide; the smallest cathedral in England, it is also the college chapel of Christ Church

Tel: (01865) 276154

The Augustinian priory that once stood on this site was dissolved by Cardinal Wolsey, and its buildings and church were incorporated into Wolsey's Cardinal College, now Christ Church. The college was founded twice, first by Wolsey in 1525 and again in 1546 after his fall from favour and subsequent death, at which time the church was designated a cathedral. Alumni of the college include Albert Einstein, William Gladstone and twelve other British Prime Ministers.

Pembroke Castle
Pembroke, Dyfed

1. Ruin
2. Built: 1189-1245
3. Built for: William Marshall, Earl of Pembroke
4. Features: 75ft high round keep with 19ft thick walls; surrounded on three sides by water
5. Other: Taken by Cromwell, Civil War 1648 after a seven week siege; Henry II spent Easter 1172 here; birth of Henry VII, 28 Jan 1457; Henry VII spent 15 years of his childhood here and later made the future Henry VIII Earl of Pembroke

Owner: Pembroke Castle Trust
Tel: (01646) 681510

At the outbreak of the Civil War Pembroke became the only Welsh town to support the Parliamentary cause and held out against repeated Royalist attacks. However in 1648, by which time Parliament had all but won the war, the Mayor switched allegiance and raised an army at the castle on behalf of the king. Cromwell himself arrived to conduct the siege, and described the rebels as "a very desperate enemy, very many of them gentlemen of quality and thoroughly resolved, and one of the strongest places in the country".

Pendennis Castle
1 mile SE of Falmouth, Cornwall

1. Uninhabited
2. Built: 1544-46
3. Built for: Henry VIII
4. Features: Guards Falmouth harbour entrance
5. Other: Besieged and captured during the Civil War, 1646 - held out for 6 months under Col Arundell; apart from Raglan, which resisted two days longer, Pendennis was the last castle in Britain to surrender to Cromwell

Owner: English Heritage
Tel: (01326) 316594

Pendennis is the partner of St Mawes Castle, both built as sea defences guarding the entrance to Falmouth harbour, but Pendennis withstood a Civil War siege for much longer then St Mawes because of its strong position on much higher ground, dominating the entire peninsula.

Penrhyn Castle
1 mile E of Bangor, Gwynedd

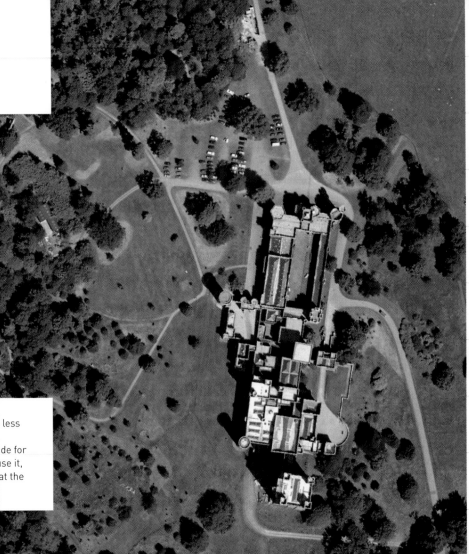

1. Inhabited
2. Built: 1820-45
3. Built by: Thomas Hopper
4. Features: Paintings by Gainsborough, Rembrandt and Canaletto; boundary wall seven miles long
5. Other: George Dawkins Pennant used the sugar and slate fortune of his anti-abolitionist great-great-uncle to build the castle

Owner: National Trust
Tel: (01248) 353084

Being a 19th century creation, Penrhyn Castle is less famous for any military distinction than for its furniture, which includes a one ton slate bed made for Queen Victoria's visit, although she declined to use it, and a decorated brass bed made for Edward VII at the then-enormous cost of £600.

Peterborough Cathedral
Peterborough, Cambs

1. Built: 12th/13th century and 1496-1508
2. Dedicated to: St Peter, St Paul and St Andrew
3. Architect: John Wastell, restored by Blore
4. Height of tower: 143ft
5. Features: 13th-century painted ceiling of vault; 13th-century West Front 85ft high
6. Other: Tomb of Catherine of Aragon; made a cathedral by Henry VIII at the Reformation; central tower rebuilt by JL Pearson, 1883-86

Tel: (01733) 343342

In the nave of Peterborough Cathedral is a memorial to a 16th century verger called Old Scarlett, with an inscription which begins: "You see old Scarlett's picture stand on high,/ But at your feet doth his body lye". He is also referred to in the parish records: "being a poor old man, and rising often in the night to toll the bells for sick persons, the weather being grievous, and in consideration of his good service, towards a gown to keep him warm, 8 shillings".

Portchester Castle
Portchester, Hampshire

1. Ruin
2. Built: Roman/c1120
3. Built for: Appropriated by Henry II
4. Features: The most complete Roman walls in Europe
5. Other: Henry V embarked here for Agincourt in 1415; Henry VIII courted Anne Boleyn here; used as a prison camp for French prisoners of war in the 18th century

Owner: English Heritage
Tel: 02392 378291

This Norman castle was built in the north-west corner of a Roman fort 1000 years older, whose walls still stand to their full height. Entrances on the east and west sides of the fort were destroyed to make way for rectangular towers guarding the entrances to the new castle, and new walls were built to the south and east, meeting the Roman walls and forming an enclosure. In 1133 an Augustinian priory was built in the south-eastern corner of the fort.

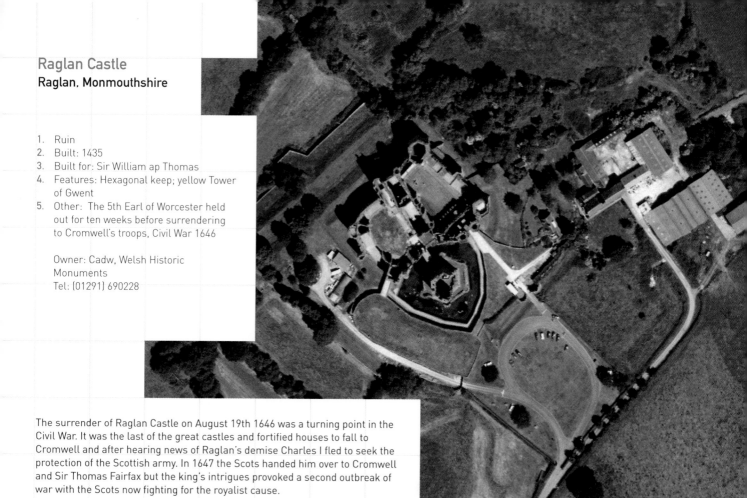

Raglan Castle
Raglan, Monmouthshire

1. Ruin
2. Built: 1435
3. Built for: Sir William ap Thomas
4. Features: Hexagonal keep; yellow Tower of Gwent
5. Other: The 5th Earl of Worcester held out for ten weeks before surrendering to Cromwell's troops, Civil War 1646

Owner: Cadw, Welsh Historic Monuments
Tel: (01291) 690228

The surrender of Raglan Castle on August 19th 1646 was a turning point in the Civil War. It was the last of the great castles and fortified houses to fall to Cromwell and after hearing news of Raglan's demise Charles I fled to seek the protection of the Scottish army. In 1647 the Scots handed him over to Cromwell and Sir Thomas Fairfax but the king's intrigues provoked a second outbreak of war with the Scots now fighting for the royalist cause.

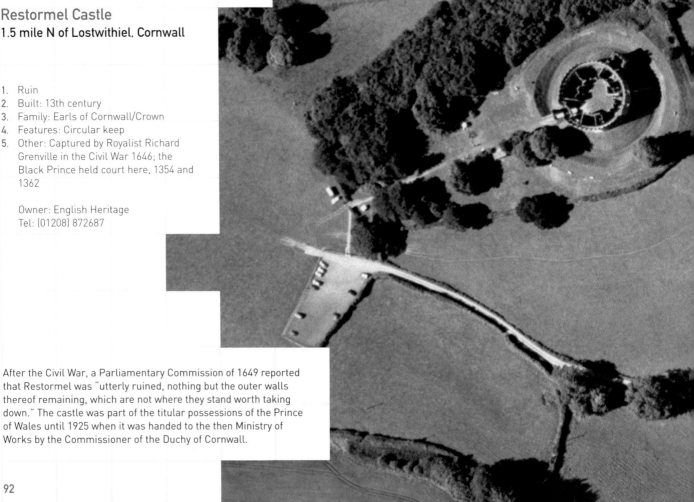

Restormel Castle
1.5 mile N of Lostwithiel, Cornwall

1. Ruin
2. Built: 13th century
3. Family: Earls of Cornwall/Crown
4. Features: Circular keep
5. Other: Captured by Royalist Richard Grenville in the Civil War 1646; the Black Prince held court here, 1354 and 1362

Owner: English Heritage
Tel: (01208) 872687

After the Civil War, a Parliamentary Commission of 1649 reported that Restormel was "utterly ruined, nothing but the outer walls thereof remaining, which are not where they stand worth taking down." The castle was part of the titular possessions of the Prince of Wales until 1925 when it was handed to the then Ministry of Works by the Commissioner of the Duchy of Cornwall.

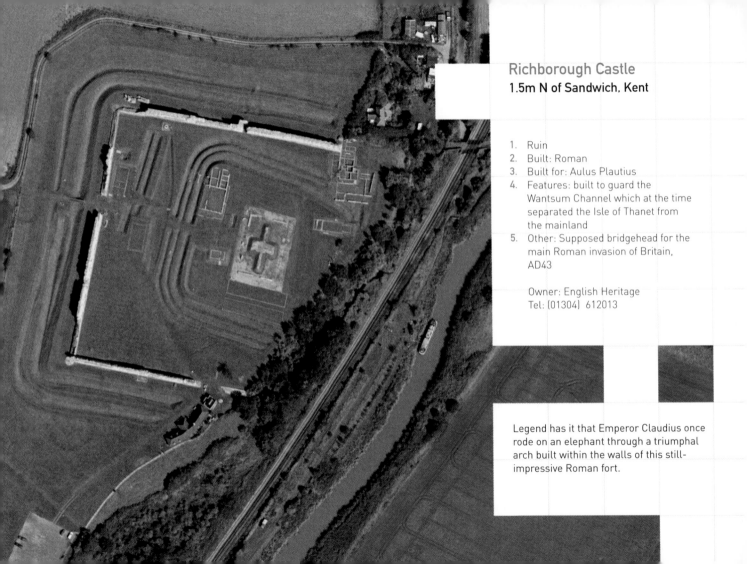

Richborough Castle
1.5m N of Sandwich, Kent

1. Ruin
2. Built: Roman
3. Built for: Aulus Plautius
4. Features: built to guard the Wantsum Channel which at the time separated the Isle of Thanet from the mainland
5. Other: Supposed bridgehead for the main Roman invasion of Britain, AD43

Owner: English Heritage
Tel: (01304) 612013

Legend has it that Emperor Claudius once rode on an elephant through a triumphal arch built within the walls of this still-impressive Roman fort.

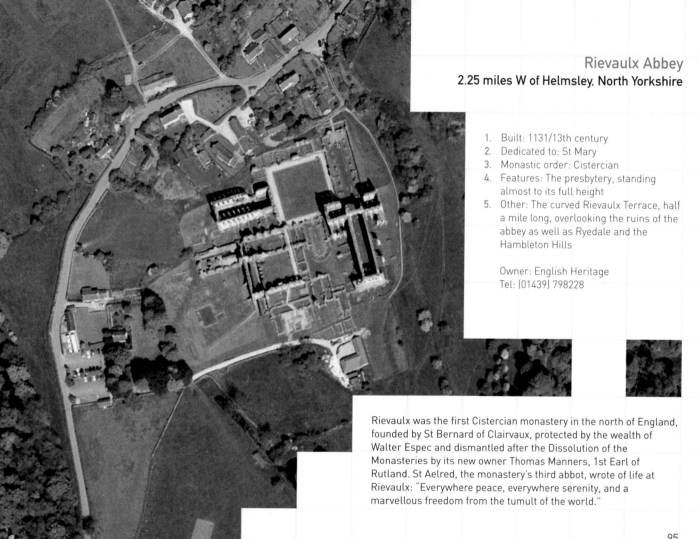

Rievaulx Abbey
2.25 miles W of Helmsley, North Yorkshire

1. Built: 1131/13th century
2. Dedicated to: St Mary
3. Monastic order: Cistercian
4. Features: The presbytery, standing almost to its full height
5. Other: The curved Rievaulx Terrace, half a mile long, overlooking the ruins of the abbey as well as Ryedale and the Hambleton Hills

Owner: English Heritage
Tel: (01439) 798228

Rievaulx was the first Cistercian monastery in the north of England, founded by St Bernard of Clairvaux, protected by the wealth of Walter Espec and dismantled after the Dissolution of the Monasteries by its new owner Thomas Manners, 1st Earl of Rutland. St Aelred, the monastery's third abbot, wrote of life at Rievaulx: "Everywhere peace, everywhere serenity, and a marvellous freedom from the tumult of the world."

Rochester Castle
Rochester, Kent

1. Ruin
2. Built: c1090
3. Built by: Bishop Gundulf of Rochester
4. Features: walls 125ft high, 12ft thick
5. Other: Successfully besieged by King John, 1215; beseiged 1264; built to defend the Medway crossing, restored by Edward III and subsequently allowed to fall into decay

Owner: English Heritage but managed by Rochester City Council
Tel: (01634) 402276

Henry I granted the castle in perpetuity to the see of Canterbury, but it turned out that perpetuity only lasted until 1215 when Archbishop Langton crossed King John. The king besieged the castle for two months before attempting to undermine it by digging out earth, propping up the walls with wooden posts and then burning the posts with vast quantities of pig's fat in order to bring down the tower. The barons then retreated behind a cross-wall but were eventually starved out.

Romsey Abbey
Romsey, Hampshire

1. Built: 907/1140-1240
2. Dedicated to: St Mary and St Ethelflaeda
3. Monastic order: Benedictine nuns
4. Features: 1858 Organ built by JW Walker & Sons
5. Other: The town of Romsey grew up around the nunnery that eventually came to be known as Romsey Abbey

Tel: (01794) 513125

After the Dissolution the townspeople petitioned Henry VIII to buy Romsey Abbey for use as the parish church. On 20 February 1544 the King signed the deed granting the building to the townspeople and parishioners for the sum of £100. Even today, 450 years on, the Abbey is the largest public meeting place in Romsey, and as well as being the centre for Anglican worship it is also used for civic occasions, school concerts, charity events, for Music in Romsey's full programme of concerts and for the three-yearly Romsey Arts Festival.

St Albans Cathedral
St Albans, Hertfordshire

1. Built: 1077-1235
2. Dedicated to: St Alban
3. Architect: Robert Mason, Hugh Goldcliff
4. Height of tower: 144ft
5. Features: 14th-century shrine to St Alban; 11th century Bell Tower; longest medieval nave in England
6. Other: St Alban was the first British Christian martyr, beheaded for protecting a priest

Tel: (01727) 860780

When St Albans Abbey was raised to cathedral status in 1877, restoration work was begun by Sir George Gilbert Scott. Unfortunately he died a year later and the work was continued from 1879 to 1885 by Lord Grimthorpe, a successful barrister and amateur architect who agreed to fund the restoration himself provided it was to his own design. In the process he added a new verb to the English language – 'to grimthorpe' is defined as 'to decorate lavishly and without taste'.

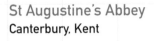

St Augustine's Abbey
Canterbury, Kent

1. Built: Norman
2. Dedicated to: St Augustine
3. Monastic order: Benedictine
4. Other: Part of the Canterbury World Heritage Site, along with the Cathedral

Tel: (01227) 767345

The original abbey was founded by St Augustine in 598, the year after he arrived in England from Rome, making it one of the oldest monastic sites in the country and arguably the birthplace of Christianity in England. The Normans demolished the original abbey and built a much larger one on the site, which was itself destroyed in the Dissolution, leaving only the ruins we see today.

St Mawes Castle
St Mawes, Cornwall

1. Uninhabited
2. Built: 1540-43
3. Built for: Henry VIII
4. Features: Clover-leaf plan
5. Other: 1646 Civil War surrendered
   without a shot being fired; part of
   coastal defences during WWI and II;
   succumbed in the Civil War because it
   was built for a sea attack and was
   therefore poorly defended on the
   landward side

Owner: English Heritage
Tel: (01326) 270526

St Mawes is the partner of Pendennis Castle, both built as sea
defences guarding the entrance to Falmouth harbour. A Spanish
raiding party arrived in Cornwall in 1595 and succeeded in burning
Penzance – garrisons were strengthened in the these castles and
others but the threatened invasion never followed, and the only
attack either castle suffered was during the Civil War, from the less
well-protected landward side.

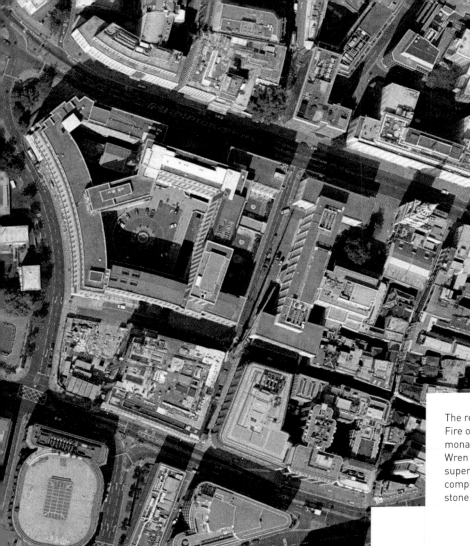

St Paul's Cathedral
City of London

1. Built: 1675-1710
2. Dedicated to: St Paul
3. Architect: Sir Christopher Wren
4. Height of cross at top of dome 366ft
5. Features: Wren's 'Great Model' of his preferred design for St Paul's; Whispering Gallery
6. Other: Tombs of Wren, Nelson, Wellington, John Donne, "Painters' Corner"; the inscription on Wren's simple tomb translates as "if you seek his monument, look around you"

Tel: (020) 7236 4128

The rebuilding of St Paul's Cathedral after the Great Fire of London in 1666 spanned the reigns of four monarchs but only one architect, and towards the end Wren was hauled up to the dome in a basket to supervise the work. By the time the cathedral was completed, Wren was too old and frail to lay the last stone, so his son performed the task on his behalf.

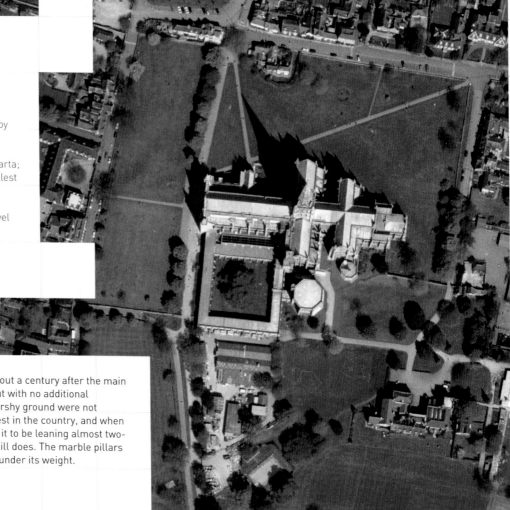

Salisbury Cathedral
Salisbury, Wiltshire

1. Built: 1220-1380
2. Dedicated to: St Mary
3. Architect: Nicholas of Ely/ restored by Wyatt
4. Height of spire 404ft
5. Features: Best copy of the Magna Carta; medieval frieze; Willis organ; the tallest spire in England, added c1330
6. Other: Painted by John Constable; inspiration for William Golding's novel The Spire

Tel: (01722) 555120

Salisbury's famous spire was added about a century after the main part of the cathedral was completed but with no additional foundations. Six foot foundations in marshy ground were not sufficient for a 6,500 ton spire, the tallest in the country, and when Christopher Wren surveyed it he found it to be leaning almost two-and-half feet to the south-west, as it still does. The marble pillars supporting the spire are visibly bowed under its weight.

Scarborough Castle
Scarborough, North Yorkshire

1. Ruin
2. Built: 12th-century keep
3. Built for: William le Gros, Earl of Albermarle & Holderness
4. Features: Built to protect the port
5. Other: Seized by Thomas Stafford 1557; besieged twice in the Civil War, 1645 and 1648; shelled by German battleships Aug 1914; George Fox, founder of the Quakers, was imprisoned here in 1665; Edward II's favourite, Piers Gaveston, surrendered the castle to the barons and was subsequently executed

Owner: English Heritage
Tel: (01723) 372451

Scarborough takes its name from a fortress (burh) built on this site by a Viking chief rejoicing in the name of Scarthi, or Scardi, a nickname meaning 'harelip' – but Scarthi's burh was not the first building on the rugged cliffs of this headland. There is evidence of an iron age settlement here, a Roman signal station and three medieval chapels as well as the Norman castle.

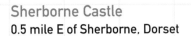

Sherborne Castle
0.5 mile E of Sherborne, Dorset

1. Inhabited
2. Built: 1594
3. Built for: Sir Walter Raleigh
4. Features: Paintings by Van Dyck, Lely, Reynolds, and Gainsborough
5. Other: The grounds were landscaped by Capability Brown in 1753; George III visited in 1789.

Owner: Digby
Tel: (01935) 813182

Sherborne provides two castles for the price of one - Sir Walter Raleigh coveted what is now known as the Old Castle but when he eventually acquired it he decided to build himself a more comfortable home, now known as Sherborne Castle, in the grounds. When Raleigh fell from the Queen Elizabeth's favour by seducing her Maid of Honour, the castle passed to the Digby family, who have lived there since 1617.

Southwark Cathedral
London

1. Built: c1213-1520
2. Dedicated to: St Saviour and St Mary Overie
3. Architect: Richard Mason
4. Height of tower 163ft
5. Features: 16th century altar screen; Choir, probably oldest Gothic structure in London
6. Other: Tomb of Edmund Shakespeare (brother of the playwright); 20th-century memorial to William Shakespeare; monument to the victims of the Marchioness disaster; the Harvard chapel commemorates John Harvard, founder of the American university, who was baptised here

Tel: (020) 7407 2939

The very thing that provided the means for the foundation of Southwark Cathedral was almost its undoing – a Thames river crossing. Tradition has it that a convent was founded here in the 7th century and that the nuns obtained revenue from a ferry across the river, but in the 19th century the east end chapel was demolished to make way for London Bridge.

Southwell Minster
Southwell, Nottinghamshire

1. Built: 1108-50
2. Dedicated to: St Mary the Virgin
3. Architect: Restored by Ewan Christian 19th century
4. Height of tower: 105ft
5. Features: "Reigning Christ" by Peter Ball;"Leaves of Southwell" in Chapter House; West Window by Patrick Reyntiens
6. Other: Raised to cathedral status in 1884

   Tel: (01636) 812649

The eagle lectern in Southwell Minster originally belonged to the monks of Newstead Abbey, who hid various valuable documents in the eagle and threw it into the lake to hide them from Henry VIII's commissioners during the Dissolution of the Monasteries. The eagle was eventually fished out of the lake by the "wicked" Lord Byron, a kinsman of the poet.

Tilbury Fort
0.5 mile E of Tilbury, Essex

1. Inhabited
2. Built: 17th century
3. Built by: Sir Bernard de Gomme for Charles II
4. Features: River-facing earthworks and landward defensive bastions
5. Other: Defended the Thames against the Dutch and the French, 17th century; location for the TV drama Sharpe; Elizabeth I reviewed her troops here before the defeat of the Spanish Armada

Owner: English Heritage
Tel: (01375) 858489

Tilbury Fort is recognised as the finest and best-preserved example of 17th century military engineering in the country, having been designed by Charles II's Chief Engineer on the site of an earlier, and smaller, Tudor fort.

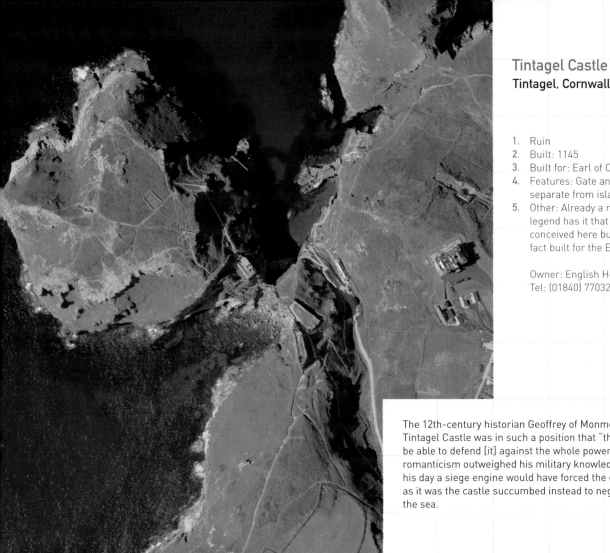

Tintagel Castle
Tintagel, Cornwall

1. Ruin
2. Built: 1145
3. Built for: Earl of Cornwall
4. Features: Gate and upper ward separate from island ward
5. Other: Already a ruin by Tudor times; legend has it that King Arthur was conceived here but the castle was in fact built for the Earl of Cornwall

Owner: English Heritage
Tel: (01840) 770328

The 12th-century historian Geoffrey of Monmouth maintained that Tintagel Castle was in such a position that "three armed men shall be able to defend [it] against the whole power of the kingdom". His romanticism outweighed his military knowledge because even in his day a siege engine would have forced the castle to surrender – as it was the castle succumbed instead to neglect and the effects of the sea.

Tintern Abbey
Tintern, Monmouthshire

1. Built: 1131/14th century
2. Dedicated to: St Mary
3. Monastic order: Cistercian
4. Features: Gothic abbey church, almost intact; remains of the Great Drain linking the buildings with the River Wye
5. Other: Wordsworth and Turner are among the writers and painters to have been inspired by the ruins of Tintern Abbey

Tel: (01291) 689251

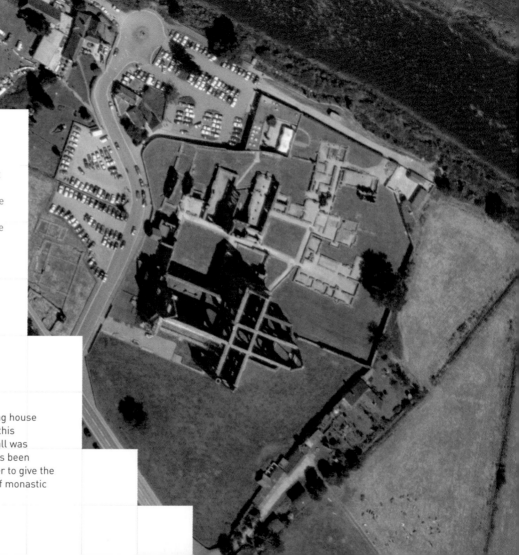

The kitchen, the infirmary and the warming house would have been the only heated parts of this Cistercian monastery, and the Novice's Hall was situated close to the warming house. It has been suggested that this may have been in order to give the novices "a falsely favourable impression of monastic life before taking their vows".

Tower of London
Tower Hill, London

1. Inhabited
2. Built: 1078
3. Built for: William the Conqueror
4. Features: Crown Jewels; White Tower, Bloody Tower, Traitor's Gate
5. Other: Haunted by Thomas à Becket, Anne Boleyn, Lady Jane Grey among many others; prisoners include: Richard II, Edward I, Edward V and his brother (the Princes in the Tower), Walter Raleigh etc; the last execution was on August 14th 1941 (of a German spy); six ravens are kept here to guard against a prophecy that the monarchy will collapse if the ravens leave

Owner: Crown
Tel: (020) 7680 9004

As one American author noted, the Tower of London "is to poisoning, hanging, beheading, regicide, and torture what the Yankee stadium is to baseball".

Wakefield Cathedral
Wakefield, West Yorkshire

1. Built: 14th/15th century
2. Dedicated to: All Saints
3. Architect: 1905 additions by JL & FL Pearson
4. Height of spire: 247ft
5. Features: Crucifix and angels by Sir Ninian Comper, 1950; glass by Charles Kempe
6. Other: Memorials to the Pilkington family; the tallest spire in Yorkshire; raised to cathedral status 1888

Tel: (01924) 373923

Wakefield Cathedral has the tallest spire in Yorkshire at 247 feet. The cathedral was restored in the late 19th/early 20th century by father and son team JL and FL Pearson - as well as numerous churches the father, John Loughborough Pearson, also designed Truro Cathedral and St John's Cathedral in Brisbane, Australia.

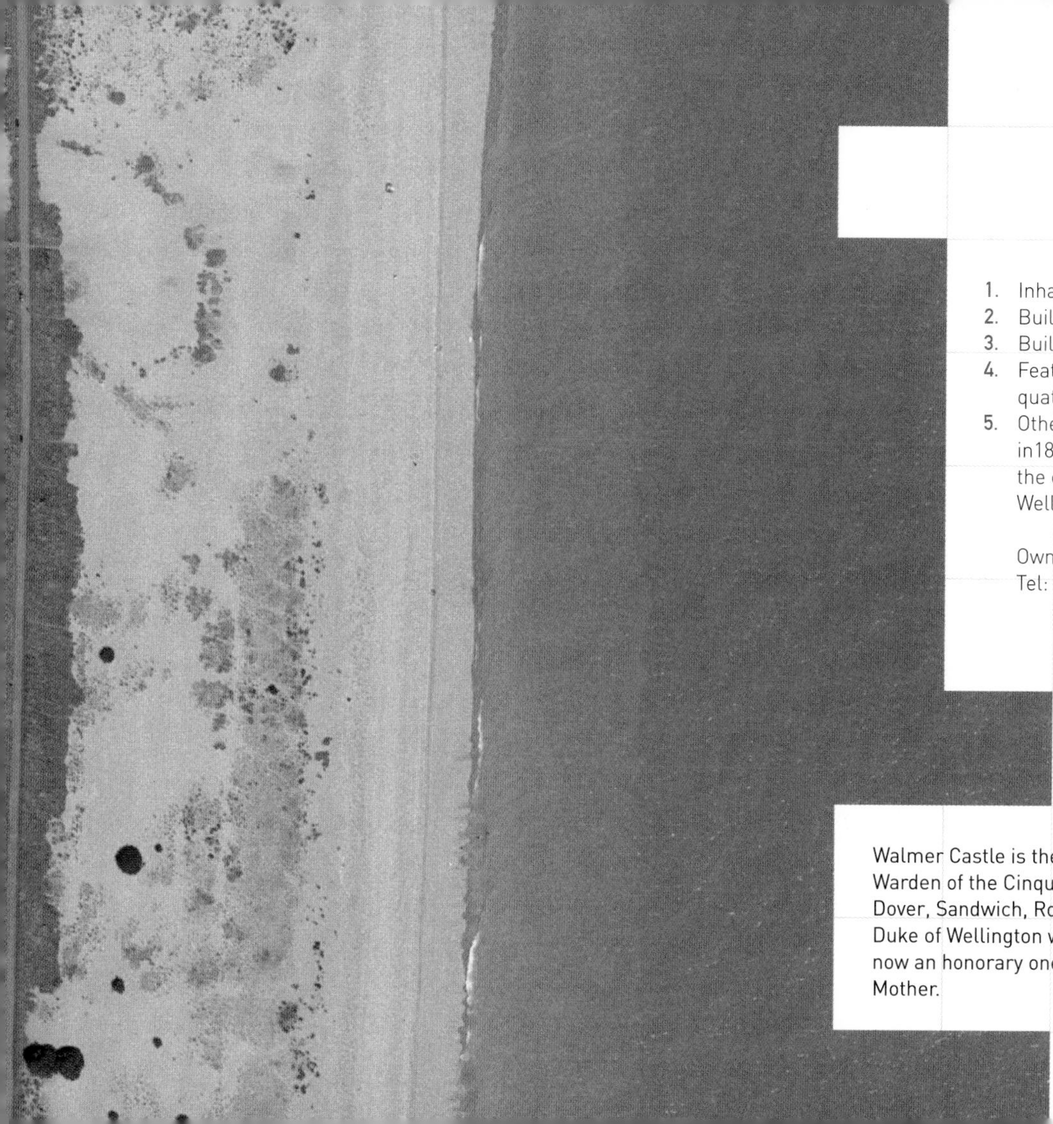

Walmer Castle
1 mile S of Deal, Kent

1. Inhabited
2. Built: 1539-40
3. Built for: Henry VIII
4. Features: Wellington memorabilia; quatrefoil plan
5. Other: The Duke of Wellington died here in1852; Wellington memorabilia include the chair in which he died and the Wellington boots he wore at Waterloo

Owner: English Heritage
Tel: (01304) 364288

Walmer Castle is the official residence of the Lord Warden of the Cinque Ports, which originally comprised Dover, Sandwich, Romney, Hastings and Hythe. The Duke of Wellington was one Lord Warden and the post, now an honorary one, is currently held by the Queen Mother.

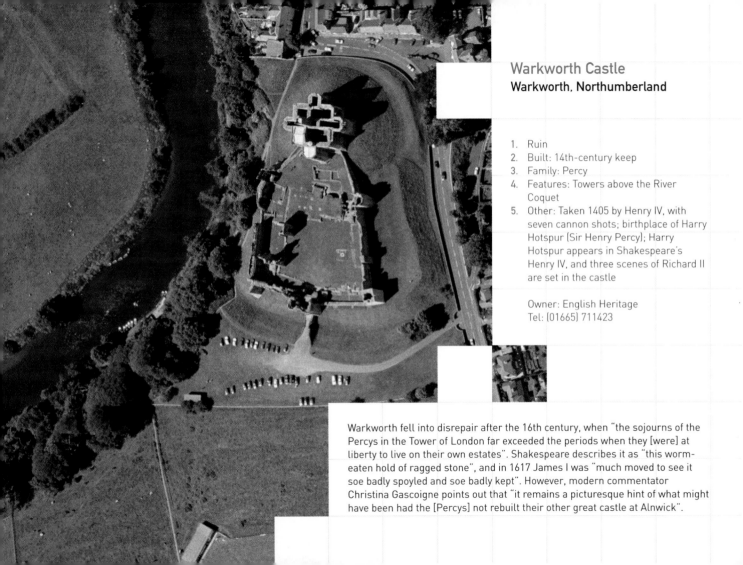

Warkworth Castle
Warkworth, Northumberland

1. Ruin
2. Built: 14th-century keep
3. Family: Percy
4. Features: Towers above the River Coquet
5. Other: Taken 1405 by Henry IV, with seven cannon shots; birthplace of Harry Hotspur (Sir Henry Percy); Harry Hotspur appears in Shakespeare's Henry IV, and three scenes of Richard II are set in the castle

Owner: English Heritage
Tel: (01665) 711423

Warkworth fell into disrepair after the 16th century, when "the sojourns of the Percys in the Tower of London far exceeded the periods when they [were] at liberty to live on their own estates". Shakespeare describes it as "this wormeaten hold of ragged stone", and in 1617 James I was "much moved to see it soe badly spoyled and soe badly kept". However, modern commentator Christina Gascoigne points out that "it remains a picturesque hint of what might have been had the [Percys] not rebuilt their other great castle at Alnwick".

Warwick Castle
Warwick, Warwickshire

1. Inhabited
2. Built: 14th century
3. Family: Beauchamp/Neville
4. Features: Warwick vase; Capability Brown parkland
5. Other: Held for Parliament by Robert Lord Brooke, Civil War; Richard Neville became known as the Kingmaker because of his military prowess in the Wars of the Roses; Madame Tussaud's has a waxworks display here on the theme of a royal weekend party

Owner: Madame Tussaud's
Tel: (01926) 406600

Warwick Castle has had its share of gruesome tales, many of them apocryphal – it is thought that Sir Piers Gaveston, Edward II's unpopular adviser and assumed lover, received summary trial in the Great Hall before his execution/murder in 1312, and that the Duke of Clarence drowned here in a butt of Malmsey wine in 1478. Sir Fulke Greville, a local MP, acquired the castle from James I and in 1621 received the title Baron Brooke, but he was killed by one of his servants before he could move in to the castle.

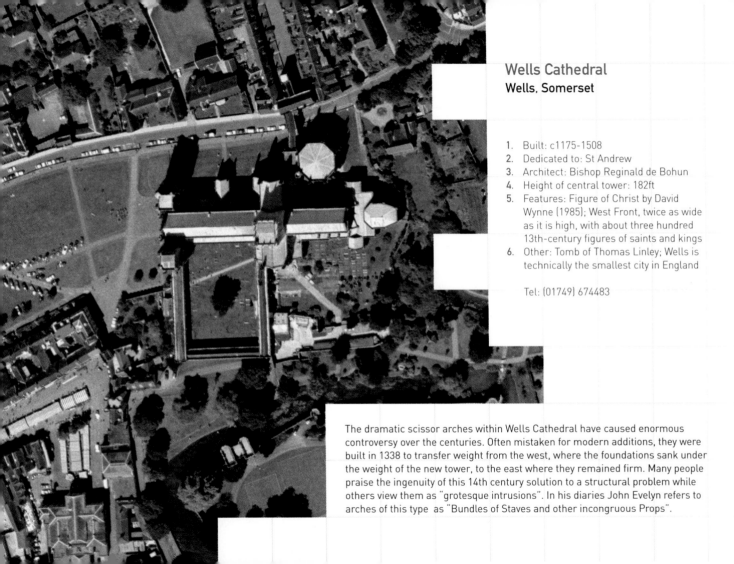

Wells Cathedral
Wells, Somerset

1. Built: c1175-1508
2. Dedicated to: St Andrew
3. Architect: Bishop Reginald de Bohun
4. Height of central tower: 182ft
5. Features: Figure of Christ by David Wynne (1985); West Front, twice as wide as it is high, with about three hundred 13th-century figures of saints and kings
6. Other: Tomb of Thomas Linley; Wells is technically the smallest city in England

Tel: (01749) 674483

The dramatic scissor arches within Wells Cathedral have caused enormous controversy over the centuries. Often mistaken for modern additions, they were built in 1338 to transfer weight from the west, where the foundations sank under the weight of the new tower, to the east where they remained firm. Many people praise the ingenuity of this 14th century solution to a structural problem while others view them as "grotesque intrusions". In his diaries John Evelyn refers to arches of this type as "Bundles of Staves and other incongruous Props".

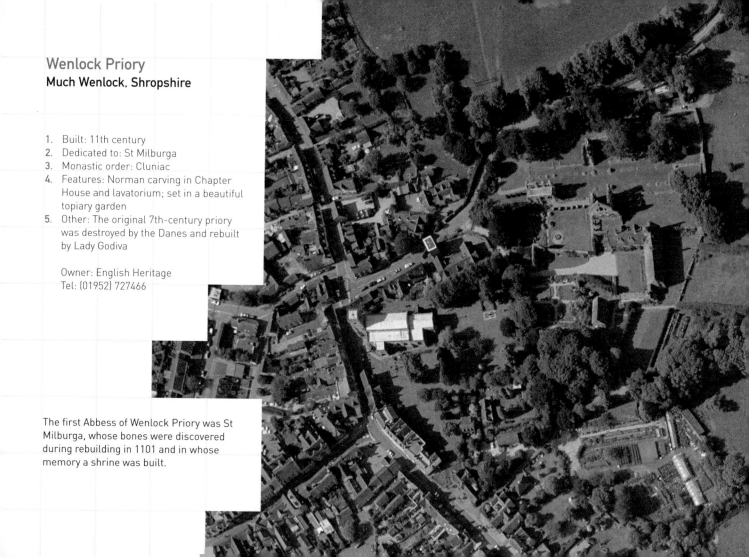

Wenlock Priory
Much Wenlock, Shropshire

1. Built: 11th century
2. Dedicated to: St Milburga
3. Monastic order: Cluniac
4. Features: Norman carving in Chapter House and lavatorium; set in a beautiful topiary garden
5. Other: The original 7th-century priory was destroyed by the Danes and rebuilt by Lady Godiva

Owner: English Heritage
Tel: (01952) 727466

The first Abbess of Wenlock Priory was St Milburga, whose bones were discovered during rebuilding in 1101 and in whose memory a shrine was built.

Westminster Abbey
London

1. Built: 1245-1532
2. Dedicated to: St Peter
3. Architect: Henry de Reyns and others
4. Height of west towers: 225ft 4inches
5. Features: Gothic nave, the tallest in Britain; tombs of royals, Poet's Corner, Musicians' Aisle; the playwright Ben Jonson was buried here standing up, to save space

Tel: (020) 7222 5152

Since St Peter apocryphally came here to dedicate the church that bore his name, what is now Westminster Abbey has been a part of British history; rebuilt by King Cnut, Edward the Confessor and Henry III, the cathedral has seen the coronation of every English monarch since William the Conqueror (except for Edward V and Edward VIII, neither of whom was crowned) and the burial of every monarch in the 500 years between Henry III and George II.

Westminster RC Cathedral
London

1. Built: 1895-1903
2. Dedicated to: Most Precious Blood of Our Lord
3. Architect: John Francis Bentley
4. Height: 284ft to top of cross
5. Features: Campanile Bell Tower; multi-coloured All Souls Chapel decorated using one hundred types of marble
6. Other: 12.5 million terracotta-coloured bricks were used in the construction of the cathedral

Tel: (020) 7798 9097

Archbishop Herbert Vaughan commissioned Catholic convert John Francis Bentley to design Westminster Cathedral, and his neo-Byzantine structure is remarkable with its green domes and stripey walls, created using courses of Portland stone amid the terracotta-coloured brick. The Campanile is dedicated to Edward the Confessor who, ironically, is buried in the Protestant Westminster Abbey close by.

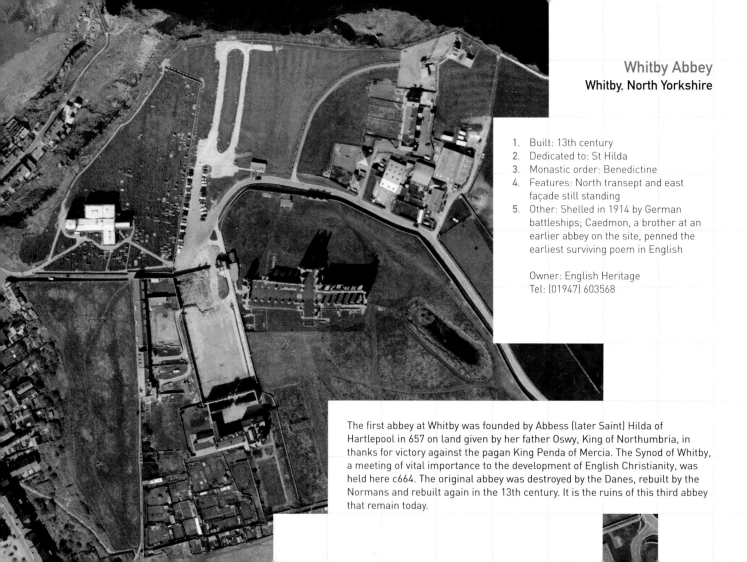

Whitby Abbey
Whitby, North Yorkshire

1. Built: 13th century
2. Dedicated to: St Hilda
3. Monastic order: Benedictine
4. Features: North transept and east façade still standing
5. Other: Shelled in 1914 by German battleships; Caedmon, a brother at an earlier abbey on the site, penned the earliest surviving poem in English

Owner: English Heritage
Tel: (01947) 603568

The first abbey at Whitby was founded by Abbess (later Saint) Hilda of Hartlepool in 657 on land given by her father Oswy, King of Northumbria, in thanks for victory against the pagan King Penda of Mercia. The Synod of Whitby, a meeting of vital importance to the development of English Christianity, was held here c664. The original abbey was destroyed by the Danes, rebuilt by the Normans and rebuilt again in the 13th century. It is the ruins of this third abbey that remain today.

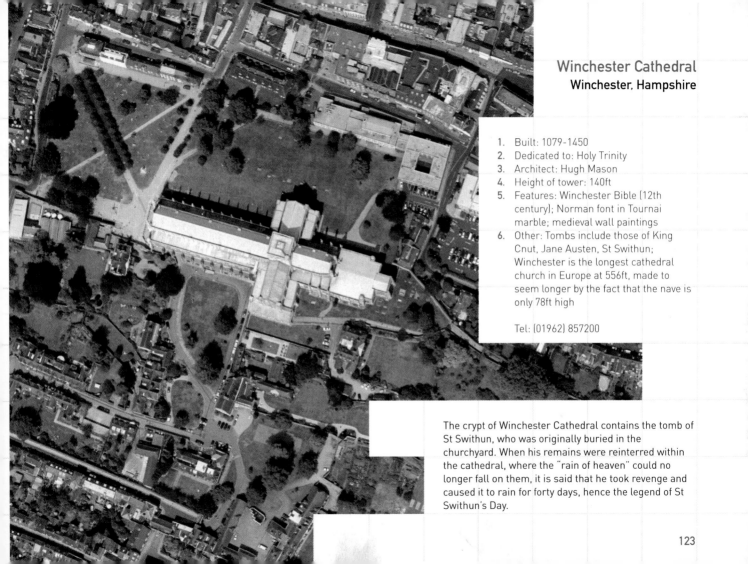

Winchester Cathedral
Winchester, Hampshire

1. Built: 1079-1450
2. Dedicated to: Holy Trinity
3. Architect: Hugh Mason
4. Height of tower: 140ft
5. Features: Winchester Bible (12th century); Norman font in Tournai marble; medieval wall paintings
6. Other: Tombs include those of King Cnut, Jane Austen, St Swithun; Winchester is the longest cathedral church in Europe at 556ft, made to seem longer by the fact that the nave is only 78ft high

Tel: (01962) 857200

The crypt of Winchester Cathedral contains the tomb of St Swithun, who was originally buried in the churchyard. When his remains were reinterred within the cathedral, where the "rain of heaven" could no longer fall on them, it is said that he took revenge and caused it to rain for forty days, hence the legend of St Swithun's Day.

Windsor Castle
Windsor, Berkshire

1. Inhabited
2. Built: c1070
3. Built for: William the Conqueror
4. Features: Queen Mary's doll's house by Lutyens; Round Tower; St George's Chapel
5. Other: Seized by Roundheads, Civil War; George III haunts the library; Kings David of Scotland, John of France, and James I of Scotland were imprisoned here;hit the headlines on Nov 20 1992 when it caught fire

Owner: Crown
Tel: (01753) 831118

Windsor is the largest inhabited castle in the world, and for nine hundred years it has been a royal residence. The castle has become an essential element of British royalty, sealed by the fact that when George V renounced his German names and titles in June 1917, he adopted Windsor as his family name. The name Windsor had already been used unofficially as a royal tag after the grieving Queen Victoria confined herself to her private apartments and became known as "the widow of Windsor".

York Minster
York, North Yorkshire

1. Built: 1154-1505
2. Dedicated to: St Peter
3. Architect: Restored by GF Bodley
4. Height of tower: 213ft
5. Features: Horn of Ulf; Great Peter bell;
   55ft high Five Sisters window; 17,000
   piece Rose window
6. Other: Tomb of Walter de Grey; struck
   by lightning 1984 causing a catastrophic
   fire; second only to Canterbury in
   ecclesiastical importance

Tel: (01904) 557216

Samuel Johnson called York Minster "an edifice of loftiness and elegance equal to the highest hopes of architecture", and its 128 windows contain an estimated half of all the medieval stained glass in England. These include the West Window, known as the "Heart of Yorkshire" for the shape of its tracery, and the East Window, the world's largest medieval stained glass window.

First published in 2001 by
HarperCollinsPublishers
77–85 Fulham Palace Road
London W6 8JB

The HarperCollins website address is:
www.fireandwater.com

Photography © 2001 Getmapping plc

Getmapping plc hereby asserts its moral right to be identified as the author
of this work.

Getmapping can produce an individual print of any area shown in this book,
or of any area within the United Kingdom. The image can be centred
wherever you choose, printed at any size from A6 to 7.5 metres square, and
at any scale up to 1:1,000. For further information, please contact
Getmapping on 0845 0551550, or log on to www.getmapping.com

A CIP catalogue record for this book is available from the British Library.

ISBN: 0 00 712230 6

05 04 03 02 01
9 8 7 6 5 4 3 2 1

Text by Ian Harrison
Design by Colin Brown
Photographic image processing by Getmapping plc
Colour origination by Digital Imaging
Printed and bound by Bath Press